NATURE,
THE
LOBSTERMAN'S
MASTER

NATURE,
THE
LOBSTERMAN'S
MASTER

BY

CHARLES W. GARNACHE

Gulf of Maine Publishing

ISBN 0-9667320-1-4

Gulf of Maine Publishing
P.O. Box 353
Biddeford Pool, ME 04006

Edited by Kathryn Garnache

Cover photographs taken by Christina Roberts

Cover designs by Kathryn Garnache

Printed in the United States of America

DEDICATION

This volume is dedicated to all those who have gone to sea before me, and to those who now go to sea with me.

CONTENTS

INTRODUCTION

Doctors, lawyers, Indian chiefs, teachers, chicken thieves, and other shady characters engage in the commercial fishery. Most people engaged in harvesting the bounty that Nature has provided are people of character. They are all highly educated like the doctors, lawyers, and schoolteachers, etc., who fish alongside of them.

The best-qualified teachers, their fathers and grandfathers, educate those without formal education. Like the football player who always looks at the camera and says, "Hi, Mom," the younger fishermen will document the accuracy of their statements by saying, "Gramps says…" If Gramps said it, then that is the final word in that discussion. The younger fishermen love their fathers, but they worship their grandfathers.

Grandfathers give grand advice. A grandson was telling me that the best advice he ever got to survive on the ocean was to know the difference between toughness and numbness.

On one occasion a couple of Gloucester men were talking on VHF channel 77. One was telling the other that he was not happy with the way his net was performing. The second asked him if he had taken it to the master net maker. He replied he had taken it to every net maker on the pier.

His friend then wondered, "Did you ask your papa?"

"Hell, no! I never thought of asking papa. He'll know what to do, and that's for sure; and if he doesn't, gramps will!"

Lobstering is an extremely hard way to make a living. One's body is stressed to its limits. There are times it is stressed beyond its limits. The lobstermen are always in pain. Trap fishing is the most dangerous occupation of them all and at times, rewarding to the soul and wallet.

Thomas Paine believed Nature was God (Deist) and if he was right, then the fishermen are in intimate contact with Nature and its Laws. To be working that close to Nature/God one is aware of the power of Nature and derives much satisfaction from the intimacy and, above all, great respect for the mandatory demands Nature imposes on all of us.

There are land people who marvel when we tell them we go out on the North Atlantic in the wintertime. Actually, the most beautiful days of the year occur in the wintertime -- not often, but sometimes. The flat calm, gray water under a sunny sky can take a person's breath away -- or is it the sea smoke and the zero temperature? Of course, winter fishing is the most dangerous.

In the summertime many lose their lives in play boats because they are not aware of the power of Nature. Their ignorance of Nature and their lack of respect cause them to do foolish things. As an example, there was the husband and wife with their two toddlers in a canoe a half mile outside Wood Island Light. This is as dangerous a spot as one can find on the ocean. It can be flat calm for more than an hour when suddenly, three monstrous breakers will come crashing over the hidden ledges. I steamed over to them and threatened to call the Coast

Guard if they didn't immediately head for the safety of the harbor.

The purpose of this work is to demonstrate the first lawmaker -- Nature. This is written into the Declaration of Independence, "...the laws of Nature and Nature's God."

Any manmade law that violates Nature's laws should be repealed by whatever means is available to the citizens. (Thomas Paine)

This is not a problem for the lobster. There is no "social scientist" or manmade laws that attempt to control its behavior. The lobster prospers in spite of the predators that constantly threaten it because Nature denies it the ability to violate its laws. The fisherman and all his land-loving fellows prosper in direct correlation to their obedience to the Laws of Nature. Violate the rules of Nature and the space shuttle would not have gotten off the ground, leave alone reached the moon -- a car would not start, planes would not become airborne, boats would not float. This we know for sure. Then why are there so many who are blind to the fact that we must subject ourselves to the dictatorship of Nature's laws?

To see God we are limited to looking at images that are created in the minds of others. To see the Laws of Nature one merely has to open one's eyes. Her splendor is a miracle in itself. Her power is obvious in rain, snowstorms, hurricanes, and tornadoes. It's also obvious in the explosion of Mt. St. Helen, and in the force of Niagara Falls. Her sweetness is seen in a sunny mid-September day in New England, and on the calm water of a mountain lake and its snow-capped peak. Her sweetness is also seen in the reflection of a full moon on a calm sea, and in a mountain meadow.

******

Freedom is the fuel that drives the economy and produces wealth. Gasoline is the fuel that gives one's car the power to function. One would not fill the fuel tank of his car with water, so then let's not let the government damage the economy by killing freedom through intervention and taxation. These are the poisons that destroy Natural Law Private Property Rights.

The Female Captain

CHAPTER I

I am the captain of the lobster-fishing vessel F/V *Kathryn Christina*. My vessel was built by Mariner Beal of Beal's Island, Maine. Mariner built it twice as strong as any pleasure boat of comparable size. This is the way all commercial fishing vessels from Maine are built. They go out in all kinds of weather, not just in July and August when it's nice enough to sit on the fly bridge and suck on a cocktail.

Our boats are workboats. They are equipped with all kinds of machinery and electronics so that we can control the vessel and make it do the work for which it was designed. However, that is the end of our control because now we come up against Nature. We are free, but we are not free!

As a commercial fisherman I have no control over the force of the wind or the direction from which it comes. The size of the seas is determined by Nature. The time of high and low tide and the direction and swiftness of the tidal currents are not mine to determine. I can only suffer, or enjoy, the consequences. When the sun is bright, making it difficult to read the electronics in the wheelhouse, I can only grin and bear it. Clear sky, overcast, fog, heat, or freezing cold are all things that Nature imposes on me day to day. These are the Laws of Nature imposed on me just as Natural Law subjects every one to its rule, like it, or not.

Out on the ocean with all its sweetness and violence I am the master. Like the paradox of humanity that is capable of great sacrifice for its fellow humans on the one hand, and of unbelievable atrocities on the other, I, on the ocean, am soothed into blissful joy on those days when the sea is at peace. Its restfulness is only disturbed by an occasional sea mammal or bird.

Then I become a raging maniac when the sea becomes violent. She strikes at me as if she is out to kill me. I fight her for all I am worth. I scream at her, "There you bitch. You thought you had me." She has struck my vessel broadside with a particularly nasty breaking sea. The fear that filled my being turns to exhilaration as I realize I beat her one more time. But my arrogance is soon subdued. I know, without any shred of doubt that her power is beyond human comprehension. Here, in her domain, she is the ruler. Her will is imposed without intelligence. Just as the Nature of water is to be wet, so then the sea is bound by Nature to be a subservient daughter.

From bow to stern, portside to starboard, I am the captain. The sea covers two-thirds of the planet. Even so, there is a great sense of security when I feel the firmness of the deck under my feet. The cockpit fences in my hundred and fifty square feet of work area so that I can move about my space as secure as walking across my living room floor. Out of the corner of my eye I can see the ocean on all sides. I know that if the few feet of deck upon which I stand were to suddenly disappear below the waves, my vessel, which was visible for miles in all directions, would then be a memory. The only reality would be overwhelming loneliness and fear. For then I would not be looking at the sea from my perch on deck, I would be alone with nothing in sight. I would be at eye level with no way to save myself. In that last moment, the strongest of my natural inclinations, survival, would go into overdrive. No matter how hopeless the situation, if there were a way to survive, I would find it. I have been on the verge of drowning three times. The greatest danger to survival, under those circumstances, is that in the last moments of consciousness the experience becomes very pleasant. One is overcome by a sense of peace, no longer aware that life is all but over. Consequently, the struggle to survive ends in a sense of euphoria.

The Spirit of Being Alive

CHAPTER II

It is odd how the greater the risk to life, the greater the sense of being alive. Commercial fishing is the most dangerous occupation. People tire of the danger. They leave to do other things, only to come back several times in their lifetime.

The fisherman is always wet and cold. Most of the time he has serious infections to his hands from fish bones. His legs and feet are killing him after long hours on a heaving deck. Yet he comes back for more. Even at an advance age, when most sane people have retired, the fishermen keep going to sea. Finally their bodies are totally broken. Willpower alone no longer forces it to function. Even then, they will take menial jobs on a boat, in a lobster pound or fish house until, mercifully, no one will hire them, and then they die. Just as General MacArthur said, "Old soldiers never die, they just fade away." So it is with old fishermen. Nature will bless them all with eternal peace.

There are those who will ask, what if God overrules
Nature and condemns them to hell and damnation for all
eternity? I would not do that no matter how much they
"sinned". Nor would any other right-thinking person.
Therefore, are we greater than God? There are things
even God cannot do. He cannot overrule Nature, for they
are one and the same. He cannot sin. He cannot create a
being superior to himself. He cannot bear false testimony,
etc.

******

It has to be pleasure! Humans and other creatures
have three natural inclinations -- survival, reproduction,
and to acquire knowledge. One could debate for a long
time as to which of the three gives the greatest pleasure.
Good food contributes to survival. One cannot reproduce
without sex, and reading is pleasurable, or one would not
bother.

"It's in their blood," proclaim those with little or no
experience at sea. It is said so many times that many
fishermen, who do not understand what drives them, begin
to believe it.

Actually it's our nature. It's the pleasure of being
in harmony with the way humans have lived even before
we were human. The way hominids, Homo Erectus and
Homo Sapiens survived. Other than the few primitive
tribes who survive to this day, we are the only truly natural
culture left. We are the lasts of the hunter-gatherers living
in civilized society. Except for the Laws of Nature, we are
as close to being free as humans can be. The only time we
have to abide by the tyranny of the clock is when we have

to keep medical appointments and the like. Do I ever hate having to be someplace at a specified time, especially because it is someone else who determines the time.

"A bad day on the water is better than a good day on land."

Miller Johnson
Biddeford Pool, ME

John Waldron, Jr., of Kittery Point, Maine, tells the story of a friend of his who has a small shop behind his house. In his shop he manufactures one product – top-of-the-line canoe paddles.

An out-of-stater visited the shop and asked how much he charged for his paddles. He was told that they were seventy dollars each. The prospective buyer thought that the price was rather high. He asked if there were any seconds available, and was told there were.

"And how much are they?" he asked.

"One hundred and forty dollars," was the reply.

"Ouch!" he gasped. "Why so much more?"

"Because there is twice the demand for the seconds," he was told.

"A rough sea is one that rolls the cream out of my coffee."

"To survive at sea one must know the difference between toughness and numbness."

Referring to his driving -- "The only thing I never hit is the State lottery."

Chink McKay
Cape Porpoise, ME

"A commercial fisherman is a fella who when he's onshore, wishes he was at sea, and when he is at sea, wishes he was home."

Author unknown

Instincts v/s Superstition

CHAPTER III

Superstition and totalitarian governments are the greatest obstacles to progress. Somewhere between the provable Laws of Nature and the existence of a spiritual power is a force no one clearly understands. There have been countless examples detailed in literature. For the most part, these stories make our flesh crawl, but they promote superstition more than they expand our knowledge. Maine is notorious for such stories, and one of the best examples occurred in the town of Kennebunk in 1842.

Old sailor Tom King was afraid. He signed on to the bark, *Isadore*, a four-masted sailing vessel, while it was being built near McCulloch's Wharf at Kennebunk in the summer of 1842. He received a month's pay in advance.

As the day neared for the *Isadore's* maiden voyage, King was bothered by nightmares. The vessel, a bark of 400 tons, seemed to have been jinxed from the start.

There had been delays about her building -- she had stuck on the ways when she was launched and had struck "Perch Rock Pier" and swung around and headed upstream.

King's dream was that he had stood on the *Isadore's* deck and looked aloft and saw all of the bark's sails blown from her yards. He had looked to the shore in his dream and saw seven coffins arranged side by side. He thought he had asked someone what the coffins were there for and was told they were "for the *Isadore's* crew."

As the day that was set for sailing, Friday, November 30, 1842, neared, other members of the crew had foreboding and dreams. Dogs howled about the home of Second Mate John Crowder for three nights in succession, and his wife tried to get him not to go on the voyage. He himself doubted whether he would ever return.

Captain Paul Grant, who booked passage on the bark to New Orleans where he was to take command of his own ship, told Captain Leander Foss when he came onboard that he had dreamt he saw a coffin under his window the night before the bark sailed.

"If my kit wasn't onboard, I would throw up the whole voyage," he said. Seaman William B. Harding stood on deck and told someone he wished the bark was a thousand miles at sea, and he, himself, was onshore.

Nevertheless, preparations were made for the departure. And at about 10:00 a.m. on November 30, 1842, the *Isadore*, with its cargo of hay, was ready to sail for New Orleans where she would load a cargo of cotton for England.

The crew consisted of Captain Leander Foss, 36; First Mate Clement P. Stone, 25; Second Mate John

Crowder, 45; Seamen Isaac C. Murphy, 23; James Young, 23; Charles Lord, 25; George T. Hutchins, 23; Alvin Huff, 23; William Thompson, 19; William B. Harding, 22; George P. Lewis, 15; Daniel Perkins, 22; Cook John Tendell, 53; and Cabin Boy George P. Davis, 18. Captain Grant went as a passenger, having been home on a visit. King, yielding to his dreams, stayed away from the bark and didn't go on the voyage.

When the time came for the bark to sail on the gloomy overcast day, an old sea dog on the dock said to Captain Foss, "Captain, I wouldn't go out today. You'll run her nose into a snowstorm, sure."

To this the Captain replied, "I'll go out today if I run her nose into hell."

So the *Isadore* sailed in the face of bad weather, which before afternoon had turned into one of the worst blizzards ever experienced along the coast. Adding to the *Isadore's* troubles as she left the dock was a swollen rudder that made the bark hard to handle. This, combined with the storm, prevented Captain Foss from working his vessel away from land.

That afternoon and night were among the wildest ever known on the coast. The next morning a peddler drove into Kennebunk from York with news. He told Leonard Webber and John H. Emery that a vessel had been wrecked at Wells during the night.

Emery and Webber drove to Freeman's Beach in Wells and were the first at the wreck. It was the *Isadore*!

The bark had been blown up on the ragged rocks, and the tide had left her firmly wedged on the ledges. Her bottom was all right, but the upper part of the vessel was stove to splinters.

The terrible force of the sea and the gale was manifest in the way the rigging was twisted and the heavy timbers splintered. Her mast had broken off short and the rigging of the masthead was twisted into big balls and jammed down among the rocks. What could be found of her sails showed the crew had hurried and made desperate efforts to save the bark, three reefs having been taken in one of the sails, but the wind had torn the sails away.

Seven of the bodies of the fifteen were recovered. There were only two who had not been terribly crushed and mangled by the water, the sharp rocks, and timbers of the wreck. Those were Tendell, the cook, and Davis, the cabin boy.

Full suits of oilskins had helped to protect them. One leg was found between the rocks, which had been broken short at the hip and torn from the body. Clement Stone was identified by his name in India Ink on one arm, but his body was headless.

King's dream had been a warning, for only seven bodies were recovered from the sea to fill the seven coffins he had seen in his dream. So the *Isadore's* maiden voyage lasted less than 24 hours, and the bark went down with the loss of all hands only eight to ten miles from her starting point.

It was one of the worst tragedies along the York county coast. (Journal Tribune by Dick Charles, 1976.)

How did Tom King and Captain Grant come to know the fate of the *Isadore*? Was it the product of an expanded will to survive? Or states of objectivity while asleep that could not be achieved when awake? Prophetic dreams are a mystery that will be solved one of these days. In the meantime, if one should experience a dream that is clearer than reality when awake, one should pay close attention to the message being conveyed. In the case of Tom, it resulted in the saving of his life!

Anyone who has experienced a prophetic dream finds every detail of the dream is as clear as any conscious experience. After a careful observation one realizes that they have seen their inner self.

There are endless stories of hospitalized individuals having "out-of-body" experiences. After by-pass surgery I had a similar experience. I found myself looking into a long tunnel. At the end of the tunnel there was a very bright light. In spite of the brightness of the light, it did not hurt my eyes. The tunnel was small and I had to crawl on my hands and knees to reach the light. Once there, I found myself on the edge of a cliff overlooking a wide beach about two miles long. The sea extended from the beach to the horizon and was a pleasant shade of light gray and was calm.

There was a small, white, ranch-type house on the beach. Flying around the house, in a counter-clockwise circle, were a large number of sea gulls. There was not a sound coming from them or the waves gently washing up on the beach. Everything was brighter than anything I had ever seen, and yet the light was soft and all encompassing and did not hurt my eyes. The haunting thing about this dream was that there was no one else on earth. I was the only person left.

I awoke to find my roommate was not in the room. I sat up and stretched as far as I could in an attempt to see up and down the hall. I fought the restrictions of the wires and tubes that were inserted into my body. The hospital was deathly quiet. I was attempting to see if there was anyone out in the hall. Suddenly two nurses rushed into the room, and when they saw me, their faces drained of color.

I knew there was no one left on earth but me. "Who are you? Where did you come from?" I asked.

"Do you know where you are?" one asked.

"Yes, Maine Med."

At this point I asked them to prove who they were and to show me a newspaper to confirm the date.

Slowly I came out of my dream state and soon was back in the world of reality.

Many of the great discoveries of nature occurred to individuals as they slept -- Kekule's benzene structure, Mendeleev's periodic table, Howe's sewing machine, Neil Bohr's model of the atom, and many more too numerous to mention.

Tom King listened to his dream and lived. Captain Paul Grant did not, and died in the wreck of the bark *Isadore*. As for me, my dream was a joy. I replay it in my mind to this day.

In order to learn how to live, one must observe the other creatures that inhabit our earth. They are free of superstitions. They do not have the ability to rationalize behavior that is in conflict with their nature. For instance, there are no gay animals except in cases when they are removed from their natural habitat and confined by man in zoos and the like. One male dog might mount another male dog; but he would just as soon mount a female dog, or one's leg. It has to be realized that dogs have evolved to their present state by human intervention. Like some humans, they kill for reasons other than feeding themselves.

A female wolf was tending her three pups near the family den. She spotted her mate standing about fifty yards from the opening to the den. He stood with his head held high and a rabbit firmly clenched in his jaws which was the product of a successful hunt. His posture was one of dominance. The ground he stood on was several feet higher than the mouth of the den. It gave him an even greater appearance of pre-eminence. He stood there as if planted, giving no sign of moving toward the den.

The female jumped to her feet and moved toward the male. Her pace was a moderate walk. Her head was held low and her tail was between her legs. It was a totally submissive posture. From her throat came a subdued whine of excited anticipation. When she was a few feet from the male, she lowered her head a few inches more and turned it so that the left side of her face was under the male's head. She now quivered all over with excitement and began to muzzle the male for several minutes. He stood like a statue and permitted her to complete a familiar ritual. After several minutes they walked to the den where the pups were given the rabbit. As the pups fed, the male and female lay side-by-side watching them. Their look was one of peace and contentment.

******

They were in harmony with their nature. Unlike humans, they could not act otherwise. Mary Tyler More comes to Maine every summer to condemn the lobstermen for their cruelty. She argues that lobsters, like "humans", are "loving" creatures and can be seen walking on the ocean floor "claw and claw".

Now in my nearly three quarters of a century, whenever I saw a lobster holding another's claw, he was in the process of detaching it from his opponent. Here, again, the lobster was conforming to his nature. Lobsters are cannibalistic. They just as soon have lobster for lunch as anything else that roams the ocean bottom.

Initiation

CHAPTER IV

My first experience on a fishing boat was when I was of preschool age. The vessel was a Hampton of about twenty feet. It was a completely open boat. There was no cuddy cabin or wheelhouse. This was in the days when powered vessels replaced the Friendship sloop as the preferred Maine workboat. I was chilled to the marrow in my bones. I crawled up to the bow and pressed my body as tightly as I could against the stem in an attempt to gain some warmth and avoid the bite of the wind. I wanted warmth. I yearned for the heat of our wood stove, or, better yet, to be in my mother's arms. In the wintertime, there have been many days since I have become a man, when I yearned for a warm fire and the comfort of my wife's body close to mine. It is when one is in bed, in his home, with his own mate that one can experience all three natural inclinations at the same time. No one can be perfectly secure all of the time. The closest thing to it is being within the confines of one's locked doors. Naked flesh against naked flesh is the finest warmth there is. Such intimacy often leads to sex and can result in pregnancy, ergo, the second precept, reproducing our own kind. In the passion of the moment, in an attempt to please each other, the skills of lovemaking are refined which results in the acquisition of knowledge.

******

On most lobster boats, the only heat comes from the exhaust pipe. It passes through the bulkhead and through the wheelhouse roof. If the bow is into the wind, the exhaust pipe will make things a little more comfortable. This is of no help to the captain. He is either hanging over the side gaffing buoys or leaning over the gunwales breaking traps aboard. That's right, they are traps, not pots. We Maine lobstermen trap lobster and cook them in pots. We also haul our traps. We do not "pull" them.

Most lobster traps that are fished are four feet in length. On each side of one end there are two nets called heads, which allow entry into the trap. When the lobsters enter through the kitchen heads, they can reach the bait and feed themselves. This part of the trap is called the kitchen because that is where we Mainers eat our meals, in our kitchens. After we have our supper, we relax in the parlor, and that is what we call the next section of the trap. The trap is designed so that it is easier for the lobster to proceed into the middle parlor and then into the end parlor, rather than move back to the kitchen head and escape.

With the trap on the gunwale and the door open the lobster's instinct to survive can become painfully obvious to a crewmember's hands. Each lobster has two eyes (the better to see you with) and two claws (the better to crush a finger or two). The fine claw has razor-sharp teeth. It can shred human flesh better than anything I have ever seen. The fine claw is very quick. If one is not cautious, the lobster will have a finger or other part of one's hand in its claw. One instinctively jerks one's hand away, which causes the fine claw to rip one's flesh.

The crusher claw can break bone. The crusher claw corresponds to molars, while the fine claw serves the same purpose as incisors. The crusher claw moves slowly. When one is bitten, it is nearly always the fine claw. But one can not take the instant it would take to determine if it is the fine claw or the crusher that has a hold of him, therefore, the knee-jerk reaction when bitten. When a lobster is hanging onto some part of the trap in an attempt to keep from being "captured", the fisherman will grab the claw that is free and squeeze it shut. This will cause the lobster to release its hold after which it can be removed from the trap without damaging it.

As the crewman begins to reach into the parlor of the trap, there is anywhere from two claws to well over twenty claws that are determined to inflict damage. It takes a well-practiced individual to empty trap after trap, all day long, and escape without injury. It is a rare day that one gets back to port with the same amount of blood that he had when he left.

The lobster has many ways to inflict pain besides its claws. It has sharp protrusions all over its body. Each horn is an effective weapon that was designed to puncture flesh. When this happens, one must force out as much blood as possible to flush the wound, or an infection will set in by the end of the day. It will rage on for more than a week and cause excruciating pain. Unlike usual infections, these are barely visible until they are completely healed. At that time, a hunk of skin and flesh, the size of a nickel, will peel off the damaged area of the hand. When I am at home and complain about the pain inflicted on me by lobsters, my wife will say, "How dare they fight for their lives." She prefers the company of wild "critters" to that of people. Red squirrels will take peanuts from her hand!

The Lobster's Right To Life

CHAPTER V

The way the lobster fights to survive causes me to conclude that, like us, he has the right to life. Humans derive their right to life based on the first precept of Natural Law. We conclude that because we have a right to life, we have a right to those things necessary to sustain that life. These are the fruits of our labor. (Our labor, not someone else's labor.) Which, in turn, constitutes our private property. We, therefore, have the right to exchange our property with anyone we please. That is what is called capitalism.

The lobster could care less about capitalism; socialism, or any other man-made 'ism'. He is the product of nature, bound to live by her dictates. He never has to worry about what other lobsters will think about his looks or his actions. Nor does he ever think about what is out of style or what will be in style next season.

But what about the lobster's right to life? If I killed another human being, I would establish that my victim did not have the right to life; and, thus, I would deny that I had a right to life. So, if I kill another creature, would I deny that any of us had a right to life?

There has to be a Law of Nature that transcends all creatures' rights to life. In my opinion, that law is the law of the jungle (Nature). Might makes right. The survival of the fittest. With these words my "liberal" friends are in a state of spasm.

If the killing of another creature in order to feed myself does not threaten another human, then the act is within the Laws of Nature. We can do this to other forms of life because we are the dominant predators. Therefore, I can trap lobsters and sell them to be cooked and eaten without suffering any pain of conscience -- even though it seems to contradict the Natural Law that gives all living things some means to survive.

The dominant rule is if my actions toward another give the witness to my act no cause to feel threatened by me, then my actions are in harmony with Nature. If the witness to my act feels endangered, then my actions lose the legitimacy of Nature and in actual fact is an act of offensive violence, which can never be justified between humans. (Natural Law and Natural Rights) -- James A Donald.

Humans, like many other creatures, are violent. Whereas offensive violence can never be justified between humans, Nature allows creatures to commit offensive violence in order to feed.

On the other hand, Nature compels us to commit defensive violence to guarantee our survival, freedom and property.

In order to maintain an orderly society, we surrender some of our freedom to government. With the absence of a general knowledge of Natural Law by citizens, this is very dangerous to the nation. There is a general uneasiness by the citizens who fear the actions of political parties in general, and governments in particular. This justified discomfort is all the proof that is needed to demonstrate that our government has strayed from the legitimacy of Natural Law to the unnatural state of force -- force being the antithesis of freedom.

The lobster does not suffer the complications of life that we humans go through. I would venture to say that there are more lobsters living off the New England coast, than people living in New England. Because they are not free to complicate their lives with endless rationalizations, they exist in an orderly fashion always obedient to their nature. There are no Republican or Democrat lobsters, and no Liberal or conservative lobsters. In fact, there are no political-type lobsters. They do not have government of any kind! I have never met a lobster that has ever met a bureaucrat. Less the reader labels me as a right-wing conservative, Republican, or something else, I should state that I am a Naturalist. I see survival through the eyes of Nature. I see myself striving for perfection by obedience to Natural Law private property rights.

The opposite of a Naturalist is a Positivist. A Positivist does not recognize or acknowledge Natural Law Private Property Rights or the laws of God. He believes in man-made law and authority. He endorses force without freedom, that is to say, tyranny!

In the lobster community there are no jails, crack houses, any potholes, or smokers. There are no traffic jams. With the hundreds of thousands of lobsters I have handled in my lifetime, I have never had a single one hold up a claw and demonstrate a gang sign.

The sad part of the whole thing is that all we have to do is follow the example of the lobster -- obey Nature -- and the whole world could live in comfort and peace and enjoy the benefits of life, freedom and private property.

MMW=NR+HE x T. -- Man's Material Welfare is equal to the Natural Resources available to him, plus the Human Effort, times the Tools he has to convert the natural resources to usable products.

The lobster has natural resources, and with the use of his physical effort, converts his resources to food. Unfortunately, the lobster's wealth will never increase because his productivity is limited by the fact that he is without tools. He will exist a thousand years from now just as he exists today.

We, on the other hand, if we obey the formula stated above, will grow in wealth. Any political program that does not agree with the stated formula is ignorance or demagoguery and will result in a loss of wealth and freedom.

The American fishing fleet is shrinking. There is a constant flood of rules and regulations that contradict the above-stated economic formula. It is George Orwell's *1984,* complete with cameras and tracking devices. By the time this work is published, along with the cameras and tracking devices, there will be a live government observer on our boats, and it is the fresh-out-of-college observer who will determine whether the boat leaves port or not. Picture the scene. Some wet-eared greenhorn will have the power to overrule the captain, and if the captain doesn't like it, the Coast Guard will be on him like ants on your jelly doughnut at the family picnic.

******

In rough weather, while I struggle to keep from crashing down on deck, or being brained by a piece of flailing rigging, the lobster is going about his business like any other day. The crashing seas that are brutalizing me have little, if any, effect on the lobster as he moves about the bottom looking for a tender morsel. And when he has fed himself, he can retire to his den and take the rest of the day off. This is not so for me. I have hours of work to do before I can head for port. And when I do, I have hours to go, while my vessel is driven skyward by a wave and then comes crashing down burying the bow under tons of water. The next wave crashes over her starboard side followed by another on the port side, just to keep things even. The next sea lifts the stern out of the water, and the boat surfs at twice the normal speed.

This can be fun during daylight when one can see the wave in front of the boat. If the bow starts to bury itself while the wave is pushing from the stern, I can immediately throttle back so as not to pitch pole or role over if she is forced sideways to the sea.

After dark this is a nightmare. The only clue to what is going on is the feel of the boat. To be on the safe side, I throttle back. I want to be sure she will not surf. It will take me longer to get back to port, but my nervous system will be in much better condition.

Upon entering the outer harbor everything comes to rest. I do not have to hold on. The boat glides through the flat-calm water, taking a little more time than it should to reach the pier. It wants to enjoy every moment of peace it can as the final leg of the journey comes to an end.

The trip ends in peace, but now I have to face the chaos and turmoil of being onshore. Who is on the pier? Is somebody looking for trouble, or is everyone in a good mood today? How about the Marine Patrol or the Coast Guard -- are they going to give me the once over?

Good, nobody is around. I worry, is the price up or down? As I head out onto the highway, I have to be alert to the speed trap that has been set up on the Mile Stretch. On the ocean I know what to expect. She conforms to her Nature. People are sneaky. You never know what to expect from them.

When, finally, I get home, there is my wife waiting to greet me with the news of the day. I hope she has had a good day. It is to be hoped that there is no new family crisis to report. There is the mail, and I can see there is a letter from the Federal Fishcrats. I wonder how much this new regulation is going to cost me to implement?

In the meantime the lobster is snug in his den. He does not worry about anything now that he is in his hideaway. He is alert to what lies outside his den, but not Iraq? Where is that? Monday night football? Never heard of it.

I thought I was free. I have to ask myself, who is free? The lobster, or me?

I am civilized. I get to enjoy all that civilization has to offer. I also have all of the distractions, confusion, chaos, violence, hates, love, passion, and on and on it goes. The lobster and all the other bottom dwellers do not have any of these concerns. They have only one thing to avoid -- being eaten! Otherwise, they are the ones that are free. It damn sure is not me.

****

Humans are the most efficient predators. From primitive persons to modern, we have the ability to kill any other creature, regardless of size, strength or swiftness. Is PETA right? Should we all be vegetarians? But vegetables are living things. They struggle to survive. When threatened by disease, they develop resistant strains after which the plant thrives. The Irish potato blight comes to mind. Though thousands of Irishmen died, the potato survived, and so did the Irishman with his charm, his music, and his contagious smile. He moved out of Ireland to survive, but Ireland itself nearly died.

******

In the final analysis, thinking and reasoning humans must surrender a portion of their Natural rights to government. The only justifiable reason for the existence of government is to *keep the peace*. In other words, government should protect Natural Law Private Property Rights from predators within our society and also protect us against foreign invaders who commit offensive violence against us.

If our government fails to do this, Nature obligates the citizens to change government by force, if necessary. The American Revolution is a good example of the citizens' rights to fight for their survival and kill the oppressors.

The distinguishing phenomenon is that as beings who can reason, the "greater good" has to be enforced. Government must protect its citizens from those who would act destructively by committing offensive violence against their fellow humans. However, government should leave those who commit defensive acts and live creatively, alone.

The fishermen work in harmony with Nature. Government laws must also be in harmony with Natural Law. Unfortunately, whereas this was true for most of our existence, it is no longer. There have been more fishermen lost to the tyranny of government than have been lost to the violence of the ocean. In the name of conservation, government limits the number of days we can go to sea. This forces fishermen to go to sea when the weather is too violent. Once they leave port, they can not turn around. If the vessel has been away from the pier for minutes, it will cost a precious "day at sea." Like George Orwel's book, *1984*, NOAA (National Oceanic & Atmospheric Administration) electronically monitors the vessel. NOAA does not monitor lobster boats, yet. Therefore, the lobstermen can turn back to port if they find conditions too dangerous to continue. If a squall comes up, the lobstermen can run for shelter. The ground-fish boats have to stay at the risk of life and limb.

The enforcement of fishing regulations that conflict with Nature's Laws has no right to be obeyed. Such rules are force and coercion and do violence to freedom. The same can be said about every human activity. The Laws of Nature have ruled Americans for two hundred years. But about fifty years ago this began to change. Alien philosophies have crept into our courts and legislative bodies. The Supreme Court, that is supposed to interpret our Constitution, has gone to the outrageous extreme of using foreign laws in its deliberations. Even worse, they have stripped us of our right to private property by ruling that the power of eminent domain can be used to take private property and transfer it to another citizen, or group of citizens, for the group's private use. (Kelo v City of New London) There is even a strong movement to transfer large areas of the ocean to Private Corporations. They will have the exclusive "right" to harvest fish that are now considered public property, to the exclusion of the public as a whole.

The lobster does not have a government that he must obey. He has to obey Nature. We, on the other hand, should obey Nature. If we do not, we will have to suffer the consequences. There are a million manmade laws that we must obey. The Laws of Nature are always right. The laws of man often lead to tyranny. If the lobster wants to build a new den, he does not have to surrender a year's labor for a permit. If his neighbors are not happy with his effort, they will drive him out -- if they are big enough to do so.

The lobster does not have to get an occupancy permit or wait for the plumbing, electrical, and landscaping inspectors. He does not have to think about zoning laws. We are told that we can't let people act this way because we would have chaos.

Dock Square in Kennebunkport, Maine, evolved exactly the way the lobsters build their neighborhoods. People come from all over the world to enjoy the charm of Dock Square. There was no government intervention in the development of Dock Square. It evolved before zoning, the EPA, and all of the other government busybody agencies were born. The sidewalks are as crowded as those in Time Square. By the way, who planned New York's Time Square? Who planned Paris, London, Rome, Red Square, and every other tourist attraction on this planet?

The same rules that applied to the lobster's environmental planning, applied to all of these places. Nowhere in America do the rules apply to those who have the right connections and money. The rules apply only to those of us who are too busy earning a living to spend a significant amount of our time in the political arena. Individuals do have the necessary intelligence to manage their property! Certainly we are as intelligent as the lobster.

The Power of Observation

CHAPTER VI

To be successful in business, science, art, agriculture, commercial fishing, professional sports, etc., requires a keen sense of observation and common sense. (Why is it called common sense when it is so rare?) With lobstering, one must learn every move a lobster makes in its lifetime. What does it prefer to eat? What is its favored habitat at different times of the year? At what depth does it seek during the different months of the year? How critical is water temperature and salinity? Should one set his traps on sand, mud, or hard bottom?

Are the lobsters that are being targeted those that stay in the same neighborhood all year? Or, are they those that migrate from near shore to several miles from shore, seeking the warmth of the Gulf Stream?

There is conflict between scientists and fishermen. The fishermen have lifetimes of experience observing sea creatures. The scientists go from the textbooks to the research vessel, hardly ever spending any time on deck on a commercial vessel. As knowledgeable as the commercial fishermen are, their opinions never become law. They can meet and discuss an issue thoroughly, and when they walk away, that is it. Scientists, who go through the same process, present their reports to lawmakers and their opinions become law regardless of how half-assed or incompetent they are because the people they are reporting to know even less than the "scientists." My contempt is for junk science, not true science. The Northwest spotted owl fiasco and the National Marine Fisheries Service attempt at regulating the New England ground fish and lobster fisheries are good examples of junk science. The outlawing of DDT because of the efforts of Rachel Carson's *"Silent Spring"* which caused the deaths of millions of children, was junk science at its worst. The global-warming hoax promises to be even more destructive.

Their attempts to save the Right whale from extinction would be laughable if it were not so tragic to the fishing community and to the whale. It is because of this that the commercial fishermen demanded that they be allowed onboard the research vessel as observers because they knew the results of their trawl surveys were flawed.

Within minutes that the research vessel's net was set, the commercial fishermen asked the research people if they were satisfied that their net was properly deployed. The research crew said that they were. Then the commercial boys told the researchers to haul back so that they could show them something. When the net came out of the water, the head rope was under the foot sweep. That meant the net was closed off like a sandwich in a ziplock bag. There was no way that a net closed off that way was going to catch anything.

It is on the basis of these kinds of tows that the government sets limits on the size of our catch. Is it any wonder that the commercial fishermen believe they are in a fight for their very survival? One must keep in mind that the struggle is for survival. And when the Captain has to sell his vessel at auction, what about his sons. The father was working toward the day when he could turn his operation over to his boys. With their heads hanging low they leave the auction with heavy hearts. Maybe they can get a job on the boat working for the new owner, and their heads droop another inch lower.

The birds hunt for food all of their waking hours. So do all the other creatures. And all the while they have to be alert to predators that are driven by nature to survive. We are the most efficient predators of all. So what is our problem? Why it's our fellow predators --humans. They have names like Hitler, Castro, Stalin, Usama Bin Laden, Napoleon, the ACLU, bureaucrats, wacky environmentalists, and they can be found in city halls, state capitols, Washington DC, and in the UN. Is this a "Catch 22", because there is one thing worse than government, and that is no government at all!

******

Our soldiers learn the art of warfare to the best of their ability so they can defend freedom and survive the struggle. So then we must arm ourselves with knowledge so that we can defend freedom with knowledge and survive the antics of those who would deny us the skills we need to survive their monstrous egos. They lust for the power to direct our lives in their image. After all, they are professionals and they have all the latest information at their fingertips. They know what is best for us. It never occurs to them that if they want to reform society, they should start with themselves.

"Everyone wants to save the world, but no one will help mama with the dishes." (Author unknown)

THE KNOWLEDGE OF ECONOMICS (NATURAL LAW PRIVATE PROPERTY RIGHTS) IS THE KNOWLEDGE OF FREEDOM. TO NOT UNDERSTAND THIS IS TO INVITE TYRANNY.

Where the Constitution Ends

CHAPTER VII

The lobstermen are acutely aware of the pain of busybody government. The Supreme Court has ruled that citizens cannot give up their constitutional rights. This does not apply to fishermen. When we leave the dock, the constitution stays there and does not go to sea with us. The Maine Marine Patrol can board my vessel anytime it wishes. They can search every square inch, even food containers. The Coast Guard and Federal Marshals can do the same. They do not need just cause, nor do they need a reason for boarding. Now with the Patriot Act, they do not even have to ask permission to come aboard -- not that they ever did. However, traditionally, one always asked before going aboard someone else's vessel.

A Boston lobsterman released his docking lines and headed for the grounds. Before he had gone a mile he was boarded by the Boston harbor police and thoroughly inspected. Ten minutes later he was boarded by the Massachusetts Marine Patrol. After getting underway from that incident, Federal Marshals boarded him. Finally, before he was even out of Boston harbor, the Coast Guard boarded him. This was the straw that broke the camel's back. With the Coast Guard still onboard, the lobsterman turned his boat around and refused to stop until he was back at his berth. Once there, he put his boat, traps and license up for sale and never went lobstering again.

In all fairness, I should point out that law enforcement at sea is several times more difficult than on land. In actual fact, without these agencies, there would be no fisheries left. This is small comfort when my goal is to haul a trap per minute and I am delayed thirty minutes to an hour.

"Here, You Try It!"

CHAPTER VIII

Many years ago when there was an active Coast Guard station at Biddeford Pool under the command of Chief Dan Farnsworth, Dan would wait at the mouth of the inner harbor for the lobster fleet to return to port. As each vessel arrived, Dan and his crew would board the lobster vessel and do a routine inspection. This was done in October, and we all knew that when the inspection was completed, we didn't have to think about it until the following year.

In those days the deck was loosely planked and not self-bailing. Whenever a tool or whatever was missing, it usually was because it had found its way into the bilge. The bilge was as foul a place as one can imagine. It was bad enough to gag a maggot. It was my observation of lobster-boat bilge's that convinced me that the green crabs, about the size of a quarter, would be the last form of life left when planet earth finally became space junk and our sun stopped giving us heat.

When a hatch was opened, green crabs could be seen scurrying about. The only way one knew they were green crabs was by their configuration. There was no way their color was visible. They were black from oil stains and bilge grime and yet they looked like they were prospering better than I!

On the day our boat was inspected, Chief Farnsworth found everything to his satisfaction until he realized that he hadn't seen a foghorn.

"Where is your foghorn," he asked my brother George.

"It's got to be here someplace," George replied.

"Well I want to see it."

"Sure, Dan," George said as he searched frantically. Finally he looked in the only place left -- the bilge. Upon opening the hatch, there it was, lying in the grime, oil, sea moss, and God only knows what other foul thing was down there. George got down on his knees, reached into the bilge and with the very tip of his fingers, picked up the foghorn and held it a few inches from the chief's face. The foghorn looked like a party horn and worked the same way. One had to put it in his mouth and blow!

"Does it work?" Dan asked as he took a step backward to get away from the foul thing.

George held it at arm's length, still between his fingertips, exposing the minimum amount of his own flesh to the bilge slime dripping from it.

"Here," he said to Dan, "you try it."

"Like hell I will," Dan replied. "Throw the foul thing overboard and see to it you get another from Goldthwait's before you come out again."

By now both crews split a gut laughing, except for Dan -- no sense of humor, I guess.

******

The *Dee Dee Mae II*, fifty-four feet, the *Cindy L*, thirty-one feet, and the *Lisa D*, thirty-five feet, were heading to sea, one behind the other. The forecast was for light winds out of the East. It was obvious by the size of the seas inside the harbor that the winds were anything, but light.

"*Dee Dee Mae* to the *Cindy L*. Cindy *L*, come back , Carl."

"Go up two, Marshall."

"Going up two."

"Yah, go ahead, Marshall."

"Carl, don't you think you should head back to port. It looks pretty nasty up ahead. Over."

"Oh, I don't know. I think my boat can handle it. I will keep going for a ways. If it gets nastier, I'll think about it. Come back."

"Suit yourself. That's not the *Queen Mary* you got there."

"No, but she's a Jonesport. They're tough."

Meanwhile, Fred Gagne, Captain of the *Lisa D*, was taking it all in and was also concerned for the safety of the *Cindy L*. As the *Cindy L* came off each chop, her bow would be inches from being buried by the next oncoming sea.

Fred keyed his mike. "Now, Carl, I don't want to tell you your business, but you really should turn back. That boat isn't big enough for what you're heading into."

"What are you talking about, Fred? This boat is damn near as big as yours. Come back."

"No, it ain't. I've got half again more tonnage than you have. But that's neither here nor there. I'll keep my eye on you. *Lisa D*, out."

"Thanks for that, Fred."

Within the next few minutes, the three vessels had reached the open sea. It was at this point that the *Cindy L* made an abrupt turn and headed for the safety of the inner harbor. She had caught a particular nasty sea and all the forward-facing windows had been blown out. Carl had been flushed against the transom, and the cockpit was partially flooded.

One does not need to sail into the "Perfect Storm" to come face to face with their Maker. Misjudging sea conditions, equipment failure, a submerged log, and God knows what else, one could find themselves strolling the ocean bottom with all of the other sea creatures.

Our survival instincts are extremely powerful, so what drives us to put ourselves at unnecessary risk? Like the old cliché, one puts themselves at risk when they get out of bed in the morning. So where is the line between getting out of bed and jumping off the roof of a thirty-story building?

The lobster is safe and cozy in his burrow. Like us, he has to venture from the safety of his home to find food. The further he is from his shelter, the greater the risk. The lobster realizes the growing danger as he moves away from the safety of his den, and all of his senses are at their maximum. What appears to be a conflict between aspects of survival actually compliments each other. The lobster has a keener sense of danger than we do. We labor under the nonsense that tragedy is what happens to someone else.

On a workboat we take all of the precautions we can. We keep several fire extinguishers located in strategic locations, a survival suit for each crew member, pumps, flare kits, careful inspection and spare parts. More important than anything else is the buddy system -- two boats keeping an eye on each other.

After doing everything we can to have a safe trip, we head out and concentrate on the job at hand. With luck we will get home safely and with a good catch. And if things don't work out, death will come quickly. Survival is our most powerful inclination, and yet we put ourselves in harms way. We have to leave the safety of the harbor to catch the lobster, and the lobster has to leave the safety of his burrow to find food. The lobster and I have to gamble that the risk we take will compliment our attempts to survive.

******

The lobster is obliged to obey Nature because his actions are limited by his instincts. Humans, on the other hand, have freewill, the power of reason. They can rationalize any kind of behavior. Just listen to a political debate. Human freedom extends to one's ability to violate Natural Law and one's instincts. That is why humans are a mass of contradictions, and their lives are complicated. Nothing is simple with humans. For instance, when the fishing is good for a few years, boats are overhauled and new pickup trucks start showing up. Wannabe's who see all of this "prosperity" start to itch to get in on the action.

One such character had a St. Pierre dory. It was not big enough for what he wanted. He thought if she had an extra six feet he would be in a better position to compete on the water. Down to the Diamond Match Co. in Biddeford he went and bought a bundle of clapboards. He then proceeded to nail the clapboards to the side of his boat, starting at the waterline, and extended them six feet beyond the stern. Using several old lobster crates he built a new transom and decked his creation with the doors he salvaged from old lobster crates. Considering he didn't put a bottom or keel on his extension, the addition acted like a drag chute, greatly slowing the boat. Needless to say, this gentleman never became a highliner, nor did he become very prosperous, for that matter. He never did end up with a new pickup truck.

******

My little brother Richard learned quite a bit about the Natural Laws of gravity. He found that things do not necessarily go straight down when gravity comes into play. It can move objects from a five-degree angle to a full ninety degrees.

In his pre-teen years, he fished a few traps in the outer harbor. He had tied his punt to the pier and placed a bushel of bait on the edge. He then went down a couple of rungs on the ladder and got aboard his boat. The tide was down, so the top of his head was even with the deck of the pier. He reached up a few inches above his head and grasped the fifty-pound basket of bait and pulled it over the edge of the wharf. His feet were no longer directly under the center of gravity of the bait container, which caused gravity to create an outward force that moved the punt and my brother Richard inches away from the pier. As the bushel of bait began to slide down the face of the pier, Richard had a death grip on the basket for fear of losing it overboard. The distance from the pier grew from inches to feet. The angle of Richard's body went from two degrees to ninety degrees at which point Richard and the bait were an infused part of the resulting splash. Schools of minnows, tinker-mackerel, and pollock escaped the intrusion in a full state of panic -- a mini fish 9/11.

Smile

CHAPTER IX

Out on the water I wave to every passing vessel -- play boats, workboats, it doesn't matter. With other workboats, I make sure they see my greeting and a big smile on my face. There are times when I am smiling at another captain, and in my mind I am saying, "Drop dead, you bastard." This guy is a snake, and I know it. He is not particularly fond of me, either, but he waves and smiles enthusiastically like we are the best of friends. I am sure he is muttering a few choice epitaphs behind his ugly grin. The reason we do not like each other is not important.

The fact is that on the ocean one does not know who is going to render assistance when one breaks down or has an emergency. What I do know is that I will be in need of help sooner or later, and so will my ugly "friend". I have no doubt that the two of us have been involved in rendering assistance and rescuing more people in life-threatening situations than the local Coast Guard group. So on the water the commercial folks remain civil. Of course, when we are safe onshore, a baseball bat might come out and be used to teach someone some badly needed manners. But for the most part, we love each other like brothers -- not like our own brothers, but brothers, nevertheless.

RODNEY GAGNE, HERO

On July 23' 2007, the National Weather Service forecasted the seas to be two to four feet and the wind to be out of the North at five to fifteen knots.

Based on this favorable forecast the lobster-fishing vessel *Kathryn Christina* headed out to sea.   After steaming for an hour and a half, we arrived at our first string of traps. The wind was now out of the Northeast and freshening. The seas were building. Obviously it was going to be a nasty day. Once again the National Weather Service got it wrong.

Our common sense told us to head back to port. With the price of fuel being what it was, it was decided to tough it out.   By mid afternoon there was more white water, than blue.   By then we were done hauling and headed home.

Our heading was north-northwest which forced us to take the seas on our starboard side.   We were then taking a serious trashing.   About a half-mile from the passage and into the harbor, a breaking sea, which nearly rolled us over, hit us. For a moment we lost all power, and the engine shut down. In the next instant the power came back on, except the starter switch and the bilge pumps were no longer operational. With the use of a screwdriver,

I crossed the solenoid terminals and was able to restart the engine. Unfortunately, after we had gone about a hundred yards, the engine quit for a second time. I used the same technique to restart the engine, again, only this time it was more difficult than the first time.

This procedure was repeated several times. The effort was a mistake, for now we were close to Whale Back Ledge. At that moment I realized that I should have set the anchor while I still had sea room. I sent Tim Roberts, my deckhand, up on the bow to set the anchor. I told him to let line out until I said to secure it to the mooring bit. On my command he did as ordered. There was not enough scope to the anchor line to guarantee that the seas would not force our vessel onto the ledge.

Whale Back Ledge extends in an easterly seaward direction. The *Kathryn Christina* was ten to fifteen feet parallel to the ledge. I kept a sharp eye on the GPS so that I would know if the anchor dragged. Breakers as high as the wheelhouse roof crashed a few feet from our starboard side. I sat on the transom and calmly observed the scene. I did not want to cause more fear to my stern man by giving the appearance that I was frightened.

In the meantime, I described our predicament to my home base and requested that she contact Rodney Gagne. About an hour later the Fishing Vessel *Lil Indian* came into view. He immediately recognized the seriousness of our predicament. He stood off our bow for a moment, and weighed his options as to how he was going to get our towline without getting entangled in our anchor line.

He timed the breakers and passed starboard to starboard in the few feet between the rocks and us! He crossed our stern and came up on our port side. The attempt to pass the towline to DJ in the stern of the *Lil Indian* failed. He repeated his previous maneuver and, that time, the attempt was successful. DJ secured the towline to the *Lil Indian,* and my helper, Tim, secured it to the mooring bit on the *Kathryn Christina.*

We tied a life ring to the anchor line and through it overboard. We considered any attempt to save the anchor to be too dangerous. At that point we held our breath and hoped that the towline would not part. If it had parted, all would have been lost, as we no longer had an anchor. The crew of the *Lil Indian* made a towline out of used pot warp (rope). Pot warp is intended to haul three and four-foot traps, not a 34-foot loaded lobster boat of several tons. The seas were tall enough to hide the two vessels from each other. The fact that the captain of the *Lil Indian* was able to successfully rescue the *Kathryn Christina* and crew without having parted the inadequate towline is testimony to Captain Gagne's skill as a mariner.

Once the *Kathryn Christina* was safe on her mooring, the engine was started, and that time it ran smooth and recharged her batteries. The automatic bilge pump switches were by-passed, and a one-hour dewatering process had begun.

In the meantime my deckhand went ashore with Captain Gagne. Once on the pier he gave Captain Gagne a hug and thanked him profusely for saving our lives.

The seamanship necessary to successfully get the *Kathryn Christina* in tow was outstanding, but even more remarkable was that he completed the rescue without having parted the towline. The crew of the *Kathryn Christina* has recommended that Captain Rodney Gagne be awarded the Coast Guard Life Saving Medal for his demonstration of courage and seamanship. His deckhand, DJ, performed admirably in making the rescue possible.

TOM BAYLEY, HERO

My obvious attempt in this manuscript is to convince the reader that the individual's overwhelming struggle to survive, under the most adverse conditions imaginable, is proof that one has the right to life. All will agree that one has the right to life. However, it is when one attempts to define the significance of the individual's right to life, that controversy erupts from every quarter.

Tom Bayley, at the time of his act of heroism, was 23 years old. He was from Pine Point, Maine. He put his life at great risk to save the lives of fellow fishermen two hundred miles off the coast of Cape Cod -- not once, but five times in a single spectacular rescue. The incident occurred on Sunday, December 12, 1982.

The *Kathleen and Julie II*, ninety-three feet in length, had been at sea for several days. It was enveloped in a blinding snowstorm. The Coast Guard had issued storm warnings. The wind was gusting to hurricane force. The seas were twenty-five to thirty-five feet in height! Under these conditions it was impossible to fish. The crew had gone several days without a hot meal. Cooking was out of the question. Conditions below were as violent as on deck.

Up in the wheelhouse, the man at the helm concentrated on keeping the bow of the *Kathleen and Julie* head on into the towering seas. The side band VHF radio came to life. It was the 120-foot *Robert* Powell out of

Rockland, Maine, radioing a distress call to the Coast Guard. They were taking on water. They were requesting pumps to dewater their vessel! In the next instant Captain James Dow radioed a Mayday. The ship was flooding at an extreme rate, and he ordered the crew to abandon ship.

The *Robert Powell* had recently come off the ways. She had been thoroughly inspected and all necessary repairs had been made. In the heavy, Perfect-Storm-type seas, a weld had ruptured. The crew had only seconds to don survival gear and activate the life raft.

The Coast Guard issued a "Pan Pan" to all vessels in the area to keep a sharp lookout and report any sightings to the Coast Guard and to assist if possible.

The crew of the *Kathleen and Julie* calculated the position of the *Robert Powell* and where the storm winds and tide could force the life raft from the last position radioed by the captain of the *Robert Powell.*

With visibility near zero the *Kathleen and Julie* steamed toward the position where they had hoped to find the life raft. All hands stared into the raging storm, not daring to blink for fear of missing the life raft.

The helmsman struggled mightily to keep the *Kathleen and Julie* on course. The seas tossed the ninety-three-foot vessel about like it was some kind of toy. After an agonizing amount of time, the life raft was spotted exactly where the crew had guessed it would be. The seas made it impossible to haul the men from the raft over the side onto the deck of the *Kathleen and Julie.*

The deck on a dragger slopes down to the water's edge near the stern. When a net is hauled back, winches haul the net up the ramp and onto the deck where it is emptied. The net is then reset for the next tow.

Tom Bayley had ropes tied to each of his ankles. The vessel was then backed up to the life raft. At that point the crew lowered Tom, head first down the ramp. He was able to get a bear hug on one of the survivors, and the men on deck hauled him to safety. To keep the vessel in position, and not swamp the life raft, was a maneuver of masterful seamanship! To be able to do that under such adverse conditions boggles the mind. This was accomplished, not once, but five times! Tom Bayley at the age of twenty-three had saved the lives of five people. Tom Bayley would never have to prove anything to anyone. He knew in his heart that he was a **man**. And everyone who knew him, knew the same thing.

Tom Bayley was awarded the Carnegie Medal, the Coast Guard Rescue at Sea Medal, and the Merchant Marine Medal. The Merchant Marine Medal, except for wartime, has been awarded twice in the past hundred years! It is awarded for instances of outstanding seamanship and bravery.

Tom Bayley's and Rodney Gagne's survival instincts are just as strong as anyone else. The soldier who throws his body on a live grenade to save his comrades has the same strong instincts. Some survive heroic acts, many do not. It seems contrary to the Laws of Nature.

******

I doubt if there is a commercial fishing vessel crew who has not jeopardized their lives and their vessel to render aid to others in distress. The fishing vessel *Lil Indian,* thirty-five feet and named after the captain's daughter, burst into flames in the outer harbor at

Biddeford Pool. A couple of vessels rushed to the aid of the *Lil Indian,* threw fire extinguishers onboard' and raced out of the way before she blew up. At the same time, the *Kathryn Christina* and a launch from the yacht club rushed to her aid. The crew had gone overboard, but the captain had so much iron in him from repairs made to him after serious accidents, that he would have gone straight to the bottom if he had abandoned ship.

While the yacht club launch, piloted by a lobsterman, rescued the men in the water, the *Kathryn Christina* pulled alongside. As the captain held his vessel against the burning boat, Louie Staples, the stern-man, jumped aboard the *Lil Indian* with the wash-down hose from the *Kathryn Christina.* He hosed down the roof of the cuddy cabin, then jumped in the cockpit and fought the fire until he had put it out. The vessel was saved and so was the captain, "Iron" Rodney.

******

In another incident the *Kathryn Christina* was put at great risk when it was taking a short cut between Beach Island and the shore. Jerry Gagne, the sternman, at the time, grabbed the captain by the arm and pointed to an urchin diver about two hundred yards closer to the shore who was in obvious distress. Jerry had spotted the diver who had been in the process of putting on his vest and tanks. The skiff the diver was standing in belonged in a swimming pool, not on the ocean. The weight of his tanks made things top heavy. The skiff flipped and the diver was in the water. We could not hear the diver screaming for aid. His flailing arms made it obvious.

"We can't get in there," Jerry said.

"We've got to try." The captain said. "Get up on the bow. Use the Nova Scotia gaff to test the depth; and watch out for ledge and boulders. We'll go in at headway speed."

It took nearly fifteen minutes to go the two hundred yards to the diver. When he was finally onboard, Jerry asked him why he didn't release his weight belt.

The diver replied, "You know what one of these costs?"

"Is it worth more than your life, you dub?" Jerry scolded. "We just put this boat at considerable risk to save your ass because you don't have brain one. When you get back onshore you'd better stay there 'cause you sure as hell will never survive on this ocean."

******

A twenty-six-foot power yacht cut across the stern of the *Kathryn Christina*. Moments later it crashed into the Libbyshears. The crew of the *Kathryn Christina* was busy picking up a string of traps to take out to deeper water. The load of traps obstructed the view of the play boat's predicament. In the next instant the VHF radio came alive with a Mayday call. The pilot of the play boat described the nature of his distress. He had hit a ledge in the Biddeford Pool harbor.

The crew on the *Kathryn Christina* knew there was no ledge in the harbor. Two other lobster boats nearby ignored the Mayday for the same reason. The captain of the *Kathryn Christina* decided that the people on the play boat didn't know what they were talking about. They said there were three lobster boats nearby. The captain figured the passengers on the play boat were looking at his boat and the other two boats fishing the same bottom. He looked around and saw the yacht anchored and in danger of being destroyed on Libbyshears ledge.

The *Kathryn Christina* immediately moved in as close as it dared, to the yacht. It could not tow the yacht because of the load of traps onboard. It would have to fasten a towline to the bow and tow by putting the boat in reverse. This could not be done because the boat would have to back into lobster buoys and would soon become disabled.

A radio call was made to the *Errin Amanda* to assist in moving the play boat out of harms way. Jeff Abbott, in a display of fine seamanship, was able to remove the play boat to deeper water. After he had determined that the play boat was not taking on water, Jeff passed the tow to another lobster boat that was heading into port.

These examples do not answer the question as to why Tom Bayley and others like him overrule their survival instincts. Our right to life, by the same token, imposes on us the obligation to respect the right to life of all other humans. It obligates each individual to promote the welfare of others to the best of their ability. Americans live by this creed. They are the most generous people on earth. They fight wars of liberation -- never to gain territory. American lives have been lost by the hundreds of thousands to promote freedom for others.

Your brother must be free or the freedom of all others is in jeopardy. As long as there is one human who suffers from hunger or tyranny, it is the responsibility of all others to rectify the injustice as best they can.

It must be an extraordinary sense of the welfare of others that causes some to put the lives of many ahead of their own. Such acts are creative functions over and above what Nature obligates us. The opposite of this is individuals who act destructively.

The life I have is mine. The life Tom Bayley has is his. The same can be said of Rodney Gagne. If they choose to risk their lives to save the life of someone in jeopardy, it is their choice, and they have every right to make that choice. There is no greater sacrifice one can make than to put one's life in jeopardy, or loose one's life, to save others.

There is no lower form of life than a suicide bomber. His remains should be gathered and buried with a dead pig! If for nothing else, this would save a multitude of virgins the indignity of having relations with a pig. Yes, of course, this is a fairy tale, but Islamic Fascists believe it to be true.

******

HE CAME BACK FROM THE DEAD!

Three brothers, who will remain nameless, were gillnetting on Tanta (Tanner), a winter fishing ground south of Portland, Maine. The temperature was below zero and the sea was covered by sea smoke . One brother was hauling the net, the second was picking fish out of the net, and the third was flaking the net in preparation to reset it. They were about two-thirds of the way to completing the day's work when one of the brothers dropped onto the deck.

The surviving two brothers went to the third brother's aid. They looked at him and could find no signs of life.

"My God!" one of them said, "He's dead." His face contorted, his mouth popped open, and his eyes grew to half-again their normal size. His brother looked as if he had been kicked in the stomach by a mule.

"We better make a run for the harbor."

"What good is that going to do, he's dead!"

"His family will be better off with a full share than us running home with a dead body."

They agreed. Their dead brother's family would be better off with a full share of the day's catch. They picked him up and took him below. They placed him in his bunk and covered him up with a woolen blanket. The heat from the engine kept the cuddy cabin as warm as the wood stove at home.

The surviving brothers went back to work handicapped now that they were short handed.

Things went well under the circumstances. The work and bitter cold took their thoughts away from the tragedy. For another hour they worked as hard as only fishermen can.

Suddenly, the brother, who had been flaking the net in the stern, froze in his tracks. The dead brother had come up from below and yelled, "What the hell is going on here."

The sun-darkened skin of the surviving brothers turned as white as a breaking sea.

"You're dead! Get the hell down below!"

"Are you two crazy? Do I look dead? Let's get done and get home. God, but I'm cold."

Biddeford-Saco-Old Orchard Beach Courier
November 27, 2003

"FISHERMEN OFFER ASSISTANCE DURING OCEAN RESCUE"

Tom Dube of Old Orchard Beach is a fifth generation lobsterman, but he is also lucky to be alive following a near fatal accident that happened last week when he was hauling lobster traps approximately three miles from the Saco coastline.

According to friends and family members, Dube, 56, was struck in the head by a metal block (two thousand pound capacity) that is used to haul lobster traps from the water. The accident happened while Dube was working with his son, Tom, Jr., on the F/V *Harvester*, a 35-foot lobster boat that is moored in Camp Ellis.

The accident happened at approximately 9:45 a.m. Monday. The father and son team was alone on the boat when the boat's snatch block broke free and swung backward. The blow knocked the elder Dube flat on his back, but he did not lose consciousness.

Unable to care for his father and pilot the boat back to shore, the younger Dube immediately radioed for help. Several fishermen in the area responded to the call, including Dean and Ellen Coniaris of Saco.

"We did not stop to think about it," said Dean Coniaris, a lobsterman and longtime volunteer rescue worker with the Saco Fire Department. "I was just hauling up a trap when the call came in, but I threw it back overboard without even looking at it, they were in trouble, and they needed our help. There was nothing else to do."

Within minutes, Coniaris reached the location where Tom Dube and his son had been hauling traps. Knowing that his boat could get back to shore faster than Dube's boat, Coniaris and his wife helped the elder Dube onto their boat.

By this time other area fishermen, including Tom Casamassa and Roger Collard were on their way to help. At the Camp Ellis pier, other fishermen gathered, waiting for the Coniaris boat to arrive.

"He refused our suggestion to have an ambulance standing by," Coniaris, a doctor, said of the elder Dube. "I knew he had a serious injury, but he kept talking and insisting that we not call an ambulance."

While the injured lobsterman held a roll of paper towels over his wound, Coniaris sped back to the pier as quickly as possible.

Coniaris was able to reach the pier some 15 minutes before Dube's boat arrived. Doctors at the Maine Medical Center told Dube that that period of time was likely the deciding factor in his survival.

"I sure am grateful for all the people who helped me," Dube told the Courier.

Carla Morin, of the Maine Lobstermen's Association said, "It just goes to show how much these people really care about one another. So many people just dropped what they were doing to help someone else."

The Key to Life Is A Good Knife

CHAPTER X

The greatest threat to one's life on a workboat is to get caught up in the gear as it is being set, and dragged overboard. On a lobster boat there can be as much as half a mile of warp (rope) on deck at any particular time. As a trawl is set, the warp flies overboard. Every few seconds, it snaps a trap into the water. Extreme caution is required to stay clear of the flailing rope and traps. For the most part, we wear oversized boots. Should we be entangled in the trawl line, the boot will easily be jerked off a man's leg and go overboard without a crewman still in the boot.

I have been caught in the gear many times with the worst result being the loss of a boot with two exceptions. The first time I was in a situation of no escape, my first thought was how to save the trap. In the microsecond that it took to process that thought, I had also drawn my knife. In the next moment, with knife on the ready, I realized that I was in great pain, as the rope had tightened around the calf of my right leg. As the realization hit home that the choice was the trap or my leg, a quick strike with my razor-sharp blade freed me. Because of my first experience, the second time it happened, I cut the line without any thought of saving the rest of the trawl. In both instances if I had been without a good knife that I could draw quickly, I would have ended up dead. That is, the first time, I would have ended up dead. There would not have been a second time!

Journal Tribune, 10/17/91
By Tom Berg.

SEA STILL BECKONS AFTER SLIM RESCUE

Norman Brazer stared out his bedroom window on Brazer Point this morning, watching the waves and thanking God he was still alive.

"I'm happy," the 50-year-old lobsterman said. "I'm so happy to be alive."

Three days ago, friends found him bobbing in the Atlantic, unconscious, close to death, with a gallon of seawater in his belly.

Somehow he survived an hour and twenty minutes in the frigid, 51-degree seas after a lobster trap line pulled him overboard.

A vest and a will to stay alive kept his head above water. A rescue by friends and fishermen and the Coast Guard kept him alive.

Brazer's ordeal began about 2:30 p.m. Monday as he set a pair of traps into the sea from his boat the *Marcia*

Beal. A float attached to the line, called a bobber or toggle, whipped around his right calf and caught under the line, yanking him to the stern. For a moment, Brazer lay trapped, wedged against the stern, as his boat motored ahead at 5 knots and the line tightened around his calf.

"I was wedged up against the stern," he said.

Brazer had to decide: Stay where he was and face the possibility his leg would be severed, or dislodge his body and go overboard? He chose the ocean.

"The boat was going away," he said. "I watched it disappear." Brazer, a 40-year veteran of the seas, who still does 50 push-ups each morning, saw Boon Island about a half mile out. The island was life; anything short of it was death.

"It looked bigger than hell," he said. "And I didn't have many options." He began swimming.

Brazer felt his limbs going numb, but ignored it. After 15 minutes, he decided to shed some gear. He kicked off his rubber boots and pulled off his rubber apron and wool jacket. On his back, he resumed swimming. He passed out fifteen minutes later.

Brazer cannot remember what happened next, but fishermen from as far south as Portsmouth cruised for the waters off Orgunquit to rescue him.

Gardner Marshall, III, a York lobsterman and friend, watched Brazer's boat pass by his with no one onboard about 3:15 p.m. Marshall called the Coast Guard in Portsmouth, N.H., then asked all fishermen within earshot to help. Brazer estimated about twenty boats moved into action.

One friend, Mark Sewall, of York Harbor, began hauling Brazer's traps to see if a line trapped him. While checking from trap to trap, Sewall saw what he thought was seaweed bobbing on the surface. As he approached, he realized it was Brazer, his head barely visible.

"I was very fortunate he found me," Brazier said. "He could have passed by."

Just after 3:30 p.m., Sewall radioed the Coast Guard: "I found him. He's alive and very cold. We've got him onboard."

Brazer said he remembers waking up on a gurney in York Hospital where doctors had pumped a gallon of seawater out of him.

"I was on my back, wrapped in a lot of towels," he said. "The first faces I saw were my wife's and my mother's."

He stayed in the hospital until Wednesday morning. Friends visited and called. "The support really touched me," Brazer said.

Somehow he avoided pneumonia, water in the lungs, or brain damage. His right calf had ballooned out to twice its regular size, and a red, welted line shows where the rope strangled his leg.

His muscles ache. But Monday, he'll return to work, return to the sea.

"I'm lying in bed right now, looking out at the sea," he said this morning.

"I feel very contented. It gives me peace of mind."

From these anecdotes it becomes obvious why, friend or foe, at sea one greets everyone with a wave and a warm smile. Like the lobster that scavengers for food many fathoms under my vessel and struggles to survive, so do I do all that I can to abide my crushing drive to survive -- for the lobster and I are slaves to the Laws of Nature.

We are free,
The lobster and me.
But we are not free,
The lobster and me

On land or sea,
Nature rules
You and me.

******

Doug Goodale fished out of Wells Harbor, Maine. His boat was a twenty-foot open punt powered by an outboard motor. To haul traps it was rigged with an auxiliary power unit that turned a driveshaft that was attached to a capstan -- a vertical revolving cylinder about the size of a gallon bleach jug. To haul a trap Doug would take a couple of turns around the spinning capstan. Then he would put the right strain on the line and hauled the line hand over hand. The trap would leave the bottom and come to the surface. When the trap broke water, he would relax the line and stop the trap from going any higher. He held it at that exact level to break it aboard. After he took the lobsters out and put in fresh bait, he would reset the trap and go to the next one to be hauled.

Very few boats are rigged this way today. We all use a hydraulically-powered device called a Hydro-Slave hauler. This device was copied from the bobbin loader on a sewing machine. If a dinner plate was placed upside down and a second plate was placed right side up on it, it would resemble the hauling plates of a Hydro-Slave system. When hauling with this system, the rope is wedged between the plates and a lever controls the speed of the trap being hauled to the surface. When the trap is in the right position to break aboard, the lever is shifted to neutral, which stops the trap in that position. With a hand on the bridle and the other on the shifting lever, the hauling process is reversed and the trap boarded. The advantage of this system is that one does not have to handle the rope hand over hand and can keep bringing traps up from the bottom automatically. The two systems could be called winches. The Hydro-Slave hauler is "safe" and the capstan is a serious hazard.

On the fateful day that would change Doug's life forever, his hand got caught between the rope and capstan. His forearm became wound around the capstan, which broke bones and tore muscle, tendons and ligaments. As this happened, his body was pulled toward the deck and the side of the boat. The power of the winch catapulted his body overboard. (There is disagreement as to whether he went completely overboard or partially over the side.) Fortunately, the hauling motor stalled and prevented any further destruction of his body. At that point he realized that he had to get back onboard or he was a dead man. However, his torn clothing and shattered arm made it impossible. Out of desperation, he drew his knife and with his good hand began to cut away his torn clothing and destroyed arm.

Most men can't pull themselves back onboard with two good arms. Somehow Doug managed to do it with one. Once onboard Doug slammed the throttle forward and headed back to Wells harbor. He radioed for an ambulance and advised that he was bleeding, but he did not explain how serious his injury was. There was a nasty sea on and he had all he could do to handle his boat with his one good arm. At one point, his boat nearly flipped. Finally, he reached the pier. The men who were waiting for him went to his aid, but in no particular hurry.

Then they saw the blood! Doug looked as if a bucket of blood had been poured over him, and the boat looked as bad as he did. The scene now turned into panic. He was heard calling for help. His voice barely audible. As the boat hit the landing, two fishermen jumped aboard and stopped the boat. They picked him up and rushed him onto the dock while another bystander took the destroyed arm and placed it with him. At the hospital he was near death, as his body was drained of blood. Torn tissue, tendons, and muscle had wrapped itself around what was left of his arm and acted like a tourniquet, which had saved his life. No amount of skill by doctors could reattach his arm.

Doug now has a bigger and safer boat with a Hydro-Slave hauler and performs all of the duties required aboard a lobster boat. He even takes his lobsters to market at the end of the day! Doug has a reputation for insisting on doing his own thing without help, but he is always there when somebody else needs a hand. Maybe someday he will be fitted with a prosthesis.

Doug and his family were the subjects of the TV show Extreme Makeover. This became controversial, as some did not believe that Doug deserved the benefits that were awarded him by the show. It could be said that Doug hasn't always been the best-behaved lad. In my opinion, that is neither here, nor there. The fact is that he had the courage and discipline to cut off his own arm in his successful effort to survive. That says a lot for the man's character.

MAN GRABS LOBSTER BOUY AND HANGS ON

As twelve-foot waves washed over his raft (Zodiac), Mark McKenney thought about death for the first time in his 31 years.

It was his will to live, along with a makeshift anchor in the form of a bobbing lobster buoy that pulled the East Boothbay man through the 38 hours he spent stranded at sea.

McKenney's adventure began on a Sunday afternoon when he left C & B Marine in East Boothbay for what he described as "a spin around the harbor".

About an hour later, the Zodiac's outboard motor stalled some 200 yards off Ocean Point in East Boothbay. McKenney began to panic as he drifted past Ram Island Lighthouse and Damariscove Island. Then he saw the lobster buoy and latched on.

"If I had not grabbed that buoy, my next stop would have been Spain or Portugal," McKenney said Tuesday after being rescued by the crew of a passing fishing boat.

Coast Guard officials said McKenney spent Sunday night and all Monday in his 14-foot, rubber Zodiac raft. They said his raft had been tied to a lobster buoy about four miles from shore, near Pumpkin Island, the last outcropping of land before the open sea. The lobster buoy itself was anchored to a string of lobster traps that were sitting on the ocean bottom.

"He had no food or water with him, just the clothes on his back," Senior Coast Guard Chief Robert Dormady said, "If he hadn't been able to grab the lobster buoy, he would be heading south right now." McKenney's sneakers, blue jeans and down jacket all were soon soaked through with salt water. Though his upper body stayed warm throughout his ordeal, his legs and feet felt "like tree trunks."

McKenney, who does maintenance work at C&B Marine in East Boothbay, was rescued shortly after 7 a.m. Tuesday by the crew of the *Nick and Andy*, a fishing vessel based in Booth Bay Harbor. The vessel was the first boat McKenney had seen since tying his raft to the lobster buoy around 5 p.m. Sunday.

"The captain (of the fishing boat) asked me, 'You got trouble?' I said, ' Yes, I've been stuck out here for two nights, and I'm freezing my butt off.'"

McKenney was transferred to a Coast Guard cutter and taken to St. Andrews Hospital in Boothbay Harbor where he was treated for hypothermia, mild frostbite and dehydration. It took hospital workers about two hours to raise his body temperature back to normal levels.

The Coast Guard said the incident underscores the importance of carrying adequate communications and signaling equipment when traveling on the ocean.

Dormady said McKenney's Raft did not have a life jacket, a wetsuit, flares or paddles. To make matters worse, he left on his excursion without telling his co-workers or parents, who were visiting relatives in Massachusetts. No one knew he was missing because Sunday and Monday are his days off from work.

But Millie Farnham, an emergency room nurse who wrapped McKenney in warm blankets and fed him warm fluids intravenously, had nothing but praise for the rescued rafter.

"He's my hero. He is one of those people who has been touched by an angel," she said.

******

The Fishing Vessel *Lil Indian* left the pier at Biddeford Pool in the pre-dawn hours and headed for the coves east of Timber Island for a day of gathering sea urchins for the Japanese market. Among the crew was Debbie Croteau, the mother of two, who weighed in at less than 100 lbs. Normally Debbie worked the stern on the lobster boat *Noella G.* She gaffed the buoys, put the line in the hauler, and broke the traps aboard. She would then open the trap's door, and while the captain took the lobsters out, she would bait the trap. Then, on the signal of her captain, she would set it back in the water. She could do all of this as fast as any 200-pound. man.

When the *Lil Indian* arrived at its "secret spot" the anchor was set and the divers went over the side. One person tended the divers from a skiff. The divers had a string of dive bags that they towed behind them as they harvested the urchins. As a bag was filled, the diver would haul the line down until the next empty bag was within reach. A diver had to be extremely careful because the rope from his string could be anywhere around him due to wave action and tide. Then there was kelp, huge single-leaf plants that grow to several feet in length, which complicated the process. It rose from the bottom and swayed back and forth by the tide and wave action and often was snarled with the diver's trailing line.

On this particular day there was more motion than normal, and about midday, what divers dread the most, happened. Her line and kelp entrapped Debbie!

She committed a near-fatal mistake. She panicked. She struggled intensely to get free of the rope and kelp. Her breathing intensified. She tried to get her knife to cut herself free, but in her state of panic she was completely disoriented. She did not know right from left, or up from down. As she thrashed about, she had dislodged her facemask! Her lungs filled with salt water. Now she was more frantic than ever, and soon everything was calm and euphoric. She was now flat on her back, limp, and being held down by her weight belt.

Meanwhile, the tender realized something was wrong. He signaled the other divers to come to the surface, and told them that Debbie was in trouble. They dove and swam with all of their strength, and within moments, found Debbie. They rushed her to the surface and had her on deck in seconds. Immediately they began CPR. After several minutes, that seemed like an eternity, she began breathing on her own and her heart began beating with a strong and regular beat.

The crew hauled anchor and headed for home at full speed. As the vessel steamed toward port, Debbie seemed to be getting stronger. She had a killing thirst, and on the way in she had consumed a full six-pack of "ginger ale". And still her thirst persisted!

When the *Lil Indian* reached the dock, Debbie seemed fine, so they loaded up the truck and with Debby onboard, headed for market. When she finally arrived home, she was still trying to quench her thirst; but by now she was feeling quite sick. She was fortunate to be able to talk to her doctor who told her to get to emergency as quickly as she could. She was a week in the hospital, four days of which was in intensive care. Her doctor wanted to put her on tranquilizers to help her cope with the trauma she had been through. He said that if she had not gotten to the hospital when she did, she would have drowned in her own body fluids. She thanked him, but refused the drugs "I'll work through this myself. I don't want to become dependent on drugs." Debby is one tough lady -- as tough as any man I have ever known on land or sea.

******

(Names have been changed in the following anecdote.)

My friend was out lobstering with his dog, a large black Labrador, when a breaking sea hit his vessel broadside and knocked him overboard. He was a pretty poor swimmer, like most lobstermen. In fact, I don't think he could swim a stroke. The boat was in gear and about to leave him behind.

At that point in time, the Lab jumped into the water and quickly swam over to his floundering "crewmate". John grabbed hold of Beauty's collar. With one look Beauty knew he would not be able to catch the *Gracie Ann*. With John in tow, Beauty headed for East Point, and soon they were on dry land. East Point is part of the Audubon trail. One of the people who were using the trail called the Coast Guard and informed them that John was safe but that his boat was still underway with no one onboard. The Coast Guard replied that the *Gracie Ann* had been boarded, and a search had been ordered to find her captain. They said they would cancel the search order and would return the boat to port.

When asked why Beauty always rode in the front seat of the family car, John would tell you, "Because he saved my life, my wife now rides in the back."

******

East Point came close to being Arnold Cote's last bout with survival. As an avid sport fisherman, he spent more time on the ocean than most commercial fishermen. He entered all of the fishing derbies and won many of them. He also held a lobster recreational license, and on this particular day he was hauling his traps at East Point. When hauling gear, one is totally preoccupied with the task at hand. With his boat broadside to the incoming seas, Arnold never saw the large breaking sea bearing down on him. It struck his boat and lifted it high on the breaking wave, flipped it over and threw Arnold thirty feet from his overturned boat. He had difficulty as the wave "ate" his glasses, hearing aid, and boots. In the few seconds it took the first breaker to do its damage, a second breaking sea threw Arnold back within reach of his overturned boat. He was able to grab the mooring cleat, and from there he fought to drag himself up on the bottom of the overturned vessel. Time and again he tried, only to fall back into the water.

The Marine Patrol, the Coast Guard, and a Coast Guard helicopter, plus several other boats were on the scene. None was able to help Arnold. Arnold waved off the helicopter. He considered the situation too dangerous to drop a swimmer into the water. Arnold still believed he could climb onto the bottom of his overturned boat.

By then Arnold had been in the 50-degree water for over 30 minutes. He tried to reach his life jacket that was secured in the bow. Finally he was able to get it out and get one arm into it when another breaker nearly tore it from his grasp. Then the wave turned his boat right side up. Unfortunately, it was swamped and useless. Somehow he managed to get the jacket on. Without his glasses, he still was able to make out the forms of two rugged-looking lads who stood at the water's edge. He then had been in the water for nearly an hour. He looked toward shore and yelled, "Here I come." He let go and managed to swim to shore. The two young men at the water's edge jerked him up and out of the water with the ease of lifting a jacket off the ground.

Then he was safe, but the most painful part of his ordeal was about to begin. Without boots he had to walk a quarter of a mile on crushed stone in his bare feet to a waiting ambulance. Spectators offered to carry him, but Arnold was too proud for that.

In the ambulance they stripped him and wrapped him in blankets. When they told him that they were about to transport him to the hospital, Arnold said "No way".

"Are you refusing transport?" he was asked.
"That's right. Just drop me off at my house," he replied.

"I don't think I can do that. I'll have to check with the Chief."

The Chief replied to the inquiry, "You've got to go right by his house to get to the hospital. Drop him off at his home."

Arnold had them stop out of sight of his house. He did not want his wife to see him get out of the ambulance. Of course, all the while his wife had been trying to contact him by radio to find out who was in trouble.

"Hi, honey, I'm home," he said as he entered the house.

THE HAPPY LOBSTERMAN

You laugh and sing,
In early spring
And you're happy with your fate.
The water's cold
The fleas are bold
They eat up all your bait.
Your heart is light
When things go right
And all the world looks swell.
Then your motor quits,
A white squall hits,
And you're two miles east of hell.

In summertime
Comes days sublime,
Then easterly winds do screech.
And summer folk
Steal your pots of oak
The minute they hit the beach.

In that shining hour
When your bait goes sour
You must not be upset.
There are lobsters there
But your traps are bare
And nothing is what you get.

The autumn days
Should win your praise,
For then the lobsters crawl.

Just when your pots
Are catching lots
A storm will smash them all.

The work is "light,"
The prospects "bright,"
And all the profits clear.
But you'd be more rich
If you'd dig a ditch
And buried all your gear.

Author unknown

Submitted to *Commercial Fisheries News,* May 1993, by Robert Dunbar, Acton, ME. It was found on a baithouse wall about 1950.

LOST MORE THAN HIS LIVING

A lobsterman I met on the dock the other day told me he had to quit fishing. He couldn't make a living at it.

He wasn't a Mainer. He had come up here to capture the "romance" of the sea. He wanted to feel free! Of course he knew there was no such thing as freedom, just the illusion of it, because he realized Nature was the boss. And he knew from all of his reading that there wasn't any better place to feel free than fishing in the Gulf of Maine.

It's a real shame, though. He missed the point of the whole thing – fishing, I mean, not freedom.

Damn if a man doesn't get the greatest feeling of freedom out there beyond the shallows -- out of sight of land. Well, maybe not completely out of sight of land, but far enough out to break the umbilical chord that separates the land things from the sea things.

Sure, feeling free is an illusion. Hell, we all know that. Just try staying out all night without checking with your wife. Then there are times when my boat comes down off a ten-foot sea and my feet feel like they are going to lift off the deck, when I think this freedom thing can be carried too far. Besides, I know everything will come out all right. And if it doesn't, I won't know the difference, and that's for certain sure.

But I'm getting away from the point. The man made a mistake! He left the sea when he should have known his life was at it's best.

Now lobstering is fine when every time you haul a trap you come up with a counter or two and a few maybes. But that's not what it's all about.

No, sir! It's hauling a trap and finding nothing in it but the bones of the used-up bait. And it's hauling two more, with the same results -- then four, eight, and even twenty and not getting a single counter out of the bunch.

It's beginning to worry that you won't make enough to pay for the fuel. Hell, you already know you're not going to be able to pay for the bait. But if only you could break even, running the boat.

It's that damned-awful feeling of maybe having to go to town and ask for a job! It's not having to work in a building where the air doesn't move and stinks like it died years ago, it's having to ask others for help – town's people at that!

But then the first trap of the next trawl breaks water and there is a two-pounder for sure! And now, if only she isn't a seeder or "V" tail.

And she's not!

Now I see I have my first counter of the day. Yes, sir, that trap does not owe me a thing.

Why I feel so good that I could lift this boat over the next swell just by pulling on the helm. Maybe my luck has changed. Let's see if the rest of this string will do as well!

Of course, it doesn't.

But it will someday!

That's the way it is with lobstering. You stay lean, "mean", and "poor".

And sometimes when I think of the way other folks have to live, it's like a cloud shutting out the sun. I have to go off by myself. My eyes get irritated. I wouldn't want others to see the lump in my throat or the tear in my eye.

Lobsters Do Not Pay Taxes!

CHAPTER XI

For me to live successfully I must understand the nature of the lobster and to know the lobster is bound to obey the dictates of Nature. It has no other choice. I, on the other hand, do not have to obey Nature. I have freewill. I am not bound by instincts alone, but if I go through life ignorant of what Nature demands, mine will not be a happy life. Every time one violates Nature, the consequences are immediate. One might not notice the penalty for a slight offense. But step off the roof of a twenty-story building, and one will fully realize that before one hits the ground, one is not a pigeon. A spoonful of water in a fuel tank might not be noticed, but a gallon of water will stop an engine.

The incentive to work is making money. Wages are a person's private property. Every time the government raises taxes, productivity declines and the economy, as whole, decreases. Incentive is damaged by a corresponding amount.

For the lobster life is simpler. He does not have to give up any part of the fruits of his labor to the tax collector. Like all wild creatures he spends all of his waking hours seeking food, and he consumes it as he finds it. We, on the other hand, labor and end up with a piece of paper. The paper is proof that we worked and allows us to exchange it for whatever it can purchase. We cannot roam around our environment and feed ourselves as we move about, although that was the way it was done in primitive times. For most people we must use natural resources and, with the use of tools and human effort we convert the natural resources to usable products. Usable products equal wealth. The lobstermen's boat, machinery, and electronics are the tools he uses to capture lobsters. Then he converts the lobsters to usable products by marketing them.

******

One cannot prove the existence of God, but the same authority exists in Nature, and one can prove the existence of Natural Law. Nature can be seen, felt, touched, and converted into wealth. The overwhelming importance of this truth is that there is a provable authority that rules humanity and all things in the universe. *Man is a servant, not a master! "Nature and Nature's God" are the masters of the universe. The sooner mankind comes to that realization, the sooner all will prosper.*

This truth must be recognized, acknowledged, and abided by. Otherwise, the only other authority is man, and man's authority inevitably leads to tyranny. Thomas Paine argued that a just law is comprised of Natural Law, plus

force.   Remove   the element of Natural Law from
manmade law, and what is left is force. Force based on
the authority of man is tyranny.

There is a substantial literature on the subject of
Natural Law, authored, for the most part, by people who
are determined to convince the student that the square peg
goes into the round hole, and the round peg, into the
square hole. To convince the student of this folly requires
reams upon reams of verbiage. The truth requires much
less effort. Mastering this fact is an essential skill required
by the majority in a free society that will promote the
survival of the individual citizens of that society.

Natural Law is primary knowledge.   It must be
mastered by a majority and acted upon if we are to
maintain a free nation. Secondary knowledge is one of the
different   specialties   that   individuals   must   master.
Everybody does not have to be a plumber for us to prosper
as long as there are enough plumbers to take care of our
needs.

The   evolution   of   the   Laws   of   Nature   is   a
fascinating subject and an absolute requirement for free
people to remain free and for those who wish to gain their
freedom.   Survival demands it.   Millions upon millions
have died at the hands of despots because they did not
know Nature's Laws or were in fear of fighting for its
establishment in their culture. Where did the founders of
our nation come up with the ideas found in the Declaration
of Independence and the Constitution?

They knew that an apple falls to the ground when it
breaks loose from the tree. They saw that water flowed
downhill and that seeds from a plant that one put into the
ground would reproduce itself. They recognized many of

the manifestations of Nature. They knew that the products of their labor were theirs and that their very survival depended upon the protection of their private property. And to take their property to give to someone else was tyranny.

From this they knew that all men are created equal with the right to "life, liberty, and the pursuit of happiness". We derive these rights from the "Laws of Nature and Nature's God."

They were familiar with the works of Thomas Paine, John Lock, Thomas Aquinas, and the multitude of Natural Law advocates of that period.

We are told that we are a nation of laws. That statement used to mean that we are a nation that is subject to the rule of Natural Law. Today we are subject to endless laws that contradict or out-and-out violate the Laws of Nature.

Many of the laws that are used to control our society do violence to the natural order. The fools who advocate the supremacy of barbarians strive to control all of Nature.

They never caught a lobster in their lives; however, they write regulations in the name of saving the resource from exploitation. They do not have a clue as to why the healthiest fishery in the world is the Maine lobster fishery.

Before any of them came onto the scene, the fathers and grandfathers of today's fishermen were the original conservationists. They developed a lobster trap that holds legal-sized lobsters and permits sub-legal lobsters to escape. When the trap is hauled onboard, the lobsters in the trap are alive and kicking. Any female lobster that is marked as a breeder is returned to the sea, and any female carrying eggs is sent back to her home. This is a small part of what we lobstermen do to keep lobsters in prime quality from the time they come out of the trap until they end up on the consumer's plate.

******

We can arrive at the same conclusions based solely on the Laws of Nature or the Commandments, one or the other, or both. An atheist can believe in private property rights, just as a theist can. How can one say our right to life is a Law of Nature when, at one time in the evolution of Nature, there was no life of any kind? Here we come upon one of the most fascinating questions of Nature. How could Nature, which is without life, be the creator of life? How could Nature, which is devoid of intelligence, be the creator of intelligence?

******

Let's take a trip back in time -- back as far as one can go. Let the magic carpet be one's bed. The room is pitch black. One's eyes are closed. One can see the furnishing of the bedroom in one's mind's eye. Now with all the power of one's mind, one begins to drive the furnishings, one piece at a time, out of the room until there is nothing left in the room. However, there is still something there, and it can't be moved. It is space. No matter how hard one tries, one cannot eliminate space. The infinite void is without any defining features of any kind. I can only conclude that the first law of nature is that it is impossible for a state of nothingness to exist.

Step outside and look up into the sky. As far as one can see, there is space. Look through the Hubble telescope. One can almost see to infinity, and there is no end, no wall, it just goes on forever! How can this be? Everything has an end -- but not space (Nature). It just goes on forever -- a million light years, a billion, a trillion, a trillion trillion light years!

******

Subatomic particles began to form a mass due to the evolution of gravity. Eventually the mass grew to the extent that internal pressure caused an atomic reaction to occur which created all of the elements now in the universe. Not only did the law of gravity cause the creation of elements, but also new laws of nature evolved which governed the actions of these elements. Of even greater importance were the results of the interaction of these new elements.

The "Big Bang" brought about the elements, but it was the big "WOW" that created life through the workings of Nature's Laws.

Bacteria, a single cell organism capable of feeding on anything, including iron, came into being. The single cell split into two, which then split into four, eight, sixteen, etc. Eventually they overwhelmed the planet and died off to a substantial degree. What was fortunate for all warm-blooded creatures was that the dying bacteria produced the oxygen that was essential to our form of life.

That is why I can say that the reason we exist is because it is impossible for us not to exist, and that the

Laws of Nature evolved just as life forms evolved. If we are to prosper, we must follow the dictates of Nature.

Nature does not have the ability to think, to reason, or to rationalize; therefore, cause and effect occur in a predictable way. Nature is without intelligence, and yet it created intelligence. Although other creatures demonstrate they have intelligence, only humans have the ability to rationalize and violate the dictates of Nature. This ability is the root cause of all the problems that plague humans. Compared to humans, all other living things have it easy.

The lobster does not have to go through the trauma of divorce or the agony of lost love.

******

When I am out at sea, I keep a wary eye on Nature. She talks to me. The sea around my boat is like the expressions on someone's face. Is she pleased, angry, or annoyed? I can hear her whisper in my ear. If I ignore her whisper, she will get louder. She is telling me to go home. She says, "Don't be a fool. I'm about to get very nasty." She is scowling. Her face is turning dark. "I can destroy this vessel in the blink of an eye."

I am tired, and her warning is all I need for an excuse to head home. At other times, she tells me what a beautiful day we are having, and her whisper sounds nearly the same as when she was warning me to get out of her space. Now she has a different look on her face. She is soft and as calm as a sleeping baby. Her scent fills my being with joy. The fragrance of tidewater as I row out to my boat, is what gives excitement to the birth of every new day. After I inspect everything -- engine coolant, oil, drive belts -- and with the engine started, I release the mooring line and my vessel glides effortlessly toward the open sea. A sense of wellbeing fills my cup to overflowing.

******

Like us, the lobster came into being by the interaction of the many Laws of Nature. To be a successful lobster catcher, I have to be an expert as to the Nature of the lobster. I cannot force it to behave in a way that makes it easier for me to find it, nor can it act contrary to its Nature.

Although the lobster is a less-complex creature than humans, its struggle for survival is parallel to ours and, therefore, is our equal within the context of the survival of their species. We must constantly be alert to threats to our safety on the highway, in the community, and in our homes. The lobster must constantly be on guard while roaming the ocean bottom so that he doesn't end up being lunch for a cod or some other predator, including his fellow lobsters.

The lobster trap looks great to a lobster. There is plenty of food and when he is inside, he can feed to his heart's content without fear of predators because they cannot get through the wire to get at him. But then along comes the lobsterman and the trap leaps from the ocean bottom and rushes to the surface like the shuttle taking off. The next thing the lobster knows, the door swings open on what he thought was his hideaway. Some big gorilla has gotten him by the back and applies hard rubber bands over his claws. Into the lobster tank he goes with a bunch of his relatives. What he thought was a safe haven turned out to be his undoing. What? That could not happen to a sophisticated human. Can you say, "identity theft"?

******

We love Nature even if we do not understand her. People spend a fortune to have a house on the beach so that they can look out over the water a few weeks of the year. Of course there has to be a fireplace so the flames can mesmerize them. Property that borders streams, rivers, lakes, and the ocean go for premium prices because the need for water, heat (fire), and vegetation is ingrained in our nature. To have these things in abundance gives people pleasure, a sense of security and warmth.

Of all the creatures on earth, the human species is the only one with the consciousness that his struggle for survival is doomed to failure. Yet only humans have the facial muscles that make it possible for them to smile.

About the best example of a person who is tuned to nature's plants, insects, and other creatures, plus a strong sense of human nature, was observed by me in a back woods country store and gas station. There were two men leaning against a coke machine -- the type of machine that had a hinged cover and was just low enough so a person could get a little bit of their butt on it. It was not the most comfortable thing to sit on, but it was much better than having nothing to rest against. One was an old man with a full head of pure white hair and a beard that matched. He must have been in his eighties, and his eyes were full of wisdom and mischief.

The younger man was about in his mid forties and was six feet tall and was as lean as any man could be. He had the looks of a logger about him. It was early October and the younger man asked, "Well, Mr. Tarbox, what kind of winter are we going to have?"

"Well now, let me think," Mr. Tarbox replied. "I see hornets are building nest close to the ground. The cornhusks are very thin, and the caterpillars have a broad stripe down their backs. So you see, young man, it's going to be an open winter."

"Well that's certainly nice to hear," replied the younger man.

"But on the other hand," Mr. Tarbox continued, ignoring the interruption, "The squirrels have built their dens high and filled them to overflowing. And the chickens have feathers thicker than I have ever seen. You'll notice the geese are already here, and the deer have eaten all of the acorns. So you see, it's going to be a very hard winter."

Before the younger man had a chance to respond, Mr. Tarbox concluded, "So you see, we really won't know until next spring, and we really won't know even then because nobody is going to remember the same!"

******

There are times that one notices a property that looks as if it should be on life support. It's brain-dead, abandoned, lonely, and sad. It is at the point where, obviously, it will not survive much longer. Its soul is gone. It is enough to bring tears to one's eyes. One can identify with the aging process that ultimately kills what was once a home, just as it ultimately kills an individual.

A fine-looking chunky lady stepped out of a big black shiny car with New York license plates. The car was next to a stone wall that was topped with barbed wire. On the other side of the wall, a farmer was putting a couple of quarts of oil into the engine of a tractor that complained about the work demanded of it in its advance years.

The fancy lady "yoo-hooed" to the farmer and asked if he could take the time to answer a few questions. He turned from his work, wiped his hands on his overalls, and walked the few feet to the wall. "What can I do for you?" he asked.

"Well," she began, "I wonder if you could tell me about that fine old house on the side of that hill." She pointed to the house that set across the road from the field that the farmer was haying. The farmer told her all about the great farm that once prospered on the side hill and how after a few generations, hard times came to the area and the younger members of the family left for better-paying town jobs.

The older folks could not manage the farm alone, and eventually it fell into its sorry state. "My what a fascinating story," she said. "Could you tell me what people do for a living after we visitors leave?"

"The same as when you're here, lady." He went on to explain that, to him at least, the tourist dollar was not the difference between life and death.

Now farmers, most generally, do not have the opportunity to talk much to people because they work alone much of the time. Oh, they have their spouses to talk to, but the spouses have heard all of the farmer's stories many times. So when at home, he is pretty quiet.

When they have the chance to talk to a stranger, they tend to go on at quite some length. This fellow was no different, and he answered all of the grand lady's questions in great detail.

Eventually, she was so impressed by the farmer's knowledge of the area and its history, she exclaimed, "Why you must have lived here all of your life!"

To which he replied, "No, not yet."

Really, It is About Sex

CHAPTER XII

Because man is a thinking animal, he cannot face reality 24/7. He must take the time to achieve oneness (Fromm), to be entertained by others, or to distract himself by engaging in creative acts -- vacationing, etc.-- which will leave his mind refreshed. To do otherwise, one would develop neurosis, become psychotic, alter his mind with drugs, become an alcoholic, or commit suicide. We find escape in a creative way or in a destructive way. One way or the other, it will happen. (Erich Fromm)

Individuals struggle with all their might to survive until, finally, death brings the struggle to an end. Nature has invested us with tremendous strength to fight to survive, not for the benefit of the individual, but for the survival of the species.

******

Adult life is one sexual experience with everything that occurs in between directed, consciously or subconsciously, toward bringing about the next sexual experience. Members of the intelligencia could find themselves debating this premise for the rest of their lives and find themselves, ultimately, in the same camp as Sigmond Freud. I can visualize the horror on their faces. It would be a sight so delightful as to defy description.

Donald Trump did not win his latest honey because of his great personality. No, it was his fortune. I would get a great deal of satisfaction if this manuscript became a success, but when one gets right down to it, I am making this effort for my wife. The stockcar driver wants to win. He applies all of his effort and skill to win. Then when the race is over, notice the gorgeous female draped on his arm. Based on my own racing experience, taking a checkered flag is better than sex, I think! Would you believe there is a thrill greater than winning one's first checkered flag? That is seeing your son win his first race! I won the jewel that is my wife because of stockcar racing.

Beauty is what pleases the senses -- a flower, a mountain view, my lobster boat, a black lab, a woman -- it takes one's breath away. And I have asthma, so I have to be very careful to avoid looking at women, especially when my wife is with me!

******

Is the inclination to reproduce (the male's striving to void his body of semen?) greater than the male's drive to survive? How many males have lost their lives by taking a bite of the forbidden fruit? It is enough to make one wonder if sex is a stronger drive than survival. Aquinas wrote that survival was our number one inclination, imposed on us by Nature; and I, for one, am not about to disagree with Thomas Aquinas.

Nature demands that we survive. Unlike other creatures that face many threats that control their population, humans can reproduce without limit. This fact brings up questions that must be answered.

Is planet earth overpopulated? If not, will it ever be? If the answer is yes, then what do we do about it? Is it possible that overpopulation could bring about our destruction? Are wars and plagues Nature's attempt to control human population?

Is not reproduction really about survival of the species, and acquiring knowledge contributes to survival?

Research is an attempt to find Natures' secrets -- that is, bits of Natural Law as yet unknown. All progress is discovering Nature's Laws and obeying them. This is how we have moved out of caves and into today's world of wonders.

The lobster lives the same today as he did thousands of years ago. His home is still a cave. What the lobster finds to eat as he searches is his private property. In the wild, if a bigger and stronger more aggressive individual comes along, then it becomes his property. However, in civil society property, once acquired through labor, has to be protected.

Abortion is a violation of Natural Law. The possibility that overpopulation might bring about the end of humanity completely changes the complexion of the debate. When the time comes, when population growth is a threat to human population, if that time ever comes, then birth control and abortion will be in harmony with Natural Law.

No couple can afford to bring about a child every nine months. Can you imagine having fifteen kids? Only illegal aliens can afford such huge families. And that is because they don't have to pay the bills. Would you believe that one-third of Americans believe government has its own money? One-third has no idea where government gets its money, and the rest of the population knows painfully well that the money comes out of their pockets. Is it any wonder that so many elections are freak shows?

The sexual relationship between lobsters is not very different from a man and a woman. When approached by a male lobster, if the female is not in the mood, she will discourage the male by tearing off one of his claws. Human females are not quite as vicious. They will claim they have a headache. One enterprising male approached his wife after she had gotten into bed with a glass of water and a couple aspirin.

"What is that for?" she asked.

"For your headache, dear."

"I don't have a headache," she snapped.

"Oh, good, then we can have sex!" he exclaimed.

When humans have sex, one of many things can happen -- pregnancy, disease, paternity suits, charges of rape, or shotgun marriages. Damn! Maybe it would be better to be a lobster!

If the lobster is very, very careful, the worst that could happen is the loss of a claw. Should he strike first, there is no threat of court action because of spousal abuse. There are no charges of rape. But like the man who looks at a scantily-clad woman with lust in his eyes, and is greeted by the female with the words, "Not in your dreams, jerk", so it is with the lobster. For the most part, the female is twice as big and much stronger than the male. She has very little need for the male in her life. Should she allow the male to deposit his sperm, she will carry it sometimes for months, before she allows it to fertilize her eggs. The eggs are carried under her tail, and they must irritate her because there is nothing as bad-tempered as an egged-out female lobster. There are times I will break a trap aboard and inside there is a big egged-out female. The remains of several smaller lobsters litter the bottom of the trap. Sometimes I think the eggers kill more lobsters than they give birth to.

Wives can be pretty tough. A friend of mine claims that one week of every month his wife is so good-natured that if he punched her in the mouth, she would run to the medicine cabinet and get the bandages for his cut knuckles. For the following two weeks, if he were careful, things would be bearable. In the fourth week, he would go to bed never knowing if he would be alive the next morning. That is a problem a lobster does not have with his female acquaintances. Being a lobster might not be such a bad deal after all! Lobsters do not have mood swings. They are always ugly!

The smaller the lobster, the more aggressive it is. That is why they are called "snappers". In human relationships, it's the female who is the snapper. The human male has it tough. He has to void his body of feces, urine, and semen. The first two are not a problem. The third is a life's work! Women, on the other hand, have to put up with juvenile males who act like every hour of every day is recess time. In spite of all the hurdles, our numbers keep growing.

The human male brain appears to be a mass of confusion when it comes down to the reproduction of our own kind. Could this be due to the way our species came into being? Was it Nature, or an act of God? Either way, one must ask where did the third generation come from? If God created Adam and Eve and they begot Cane and Abel, then Cane or Able had to bring the third generation of humans into being by impregnating their mother!

If evolution brought about the birth of our species, then the best scientific guess is that the first human was a female who originated about thirty-five thousand years ago. The second generation had to be a mating between a Homo Sapien female and a hominid, such as Homo Erectus. Even here, the third generation had to be a mating between son and mother or brothers and sisters. Is it possible that a twisted wire in our brain stem is the cause of the odd sexual acts that occur in society?

In centuries past, a mariner on a fishing vessel who needed to be disciplined would be secured to the mast and given a good lashing with a cat-o-nine-tails. But notice how a two-hundred-pound-plus male will suffer comparable pain when getting a tongue lashing from a one-hundred-pound female.

It is a mysterious function of the Laws of Nature at work. It is comparable to one man facing another in combat. One has a knife and the other has a twelve-shot handgun. Anyone would agree that this is not a fair fight! Well, so it is when a woman confronts a man. It is an uneven match of weapons. The man has the shooter, and the woman has the silencer!

Little wonder the woman is reluctant to yield a few minutes of pleasure to the male for twenty years of servitude to his and her offspring. I will bet there are a lot of women who would love to see the chastity belt back in vogue. "There, Buster, let's see you get through that!"

"Oh, are those tears I see?"

"Ouch! Punching that brick wall must have hurt."

"You got pain? Well I would think so after putting your fist through that wall"

"Oh! That's not where you hurt?"

"Love is that painful, is it? Gee, we girls don't hurt like that. But then, we have our minds on other things. You should try thinking about something else, you big dub. You would find that you would be a lot more comfortable."

Knowledge

CHAPTER XIII

A person dies and with them goes a lifetime of skill and knowledge. At the point when they have the greatest degree of expertise, they are gone. We hunger for knowledge. We thirst for it. At breakfast we read the cereal box, which we have read every morning for the past umpteen years. We read and watch TV. We talk with others every chance we get. We devour newspapers, magazines, and trade articles. We get great pleasure in acquiring knowledge. In the simpler world of the other creatures, the mothers teach their offspring to hunt for food and to defend themselves, which enables them to survive. The mothers also teach them the skills that are needed to prosper.

When lobstering, once we break the trap aboard and clean it out, we dump what is left of the old bait overboard. The gulls swoop in to fight over what we have thrown away.

We then check the sounder and the chart plotter to determine where to reset the trawl. We now head for the next buoy in the string. The gulls follow along quietly except for the few that know our buoy colors and are waiting for us. There are times in poor visibility that it is easier to find the next buoy by seeing where the gulls are congregating. When there, I will gaff the buoy and start hauling. As I haul, the gulls wait quietly on the hauling side of the boat. Even when the trap is broken aboard, they remain quiet. As the lobsters are taken out of the trap, they still don't show any excitement. But the instant a crewmember reaches for the bait bag to empty it, they explode out of the water and all hell breaks loose until the remnants of the baits are cleaned up.

This is acquired knowledge on the part of the gulls. They had to learn this when fishermen began using bait bags because herring doesn't stay on a bait spike or bait string.

When the tide is coming in over a sandy bottom, gulls can be seen stamping their feet at the water's edge as it moves in across the sand. Forty years ago they did not do this. For the longest time I wondered what they were doing. Finally, one day, I was able to determine that the gulls' actions stirred the sand at the incoming tide's edge causing seed clams to come to the surface. This action exposed them to the gulls and gave the gulls the opportunity to eat them.

The lobster has learned how to walk. As it hunts for food it moves forward across the ocean's bottom with both claws extended in front of it, ready for action when acting as a predator. But when it feels threatened, the lobster swims backward by using its powerful tail to propel it away from its enemy at surprising speed.

Prior to the electronic age, all a fisherman had to guide him was a magnetic compass. Today the wheelhouse on a commercial vessel has so many electronic devices that it looks like the star war's flight deck.

The knowledge required to make the maximum use of these electronic marvels is equal to the skills needed to find the targeted species.

The computer age has brought the same problem to every industry. The sweet part is that productivity per person has grown substantially. Greater productivity means greater wealth for everyone.

Without the vast wealth produced by those of us in the private sector, we would have to live like those in the third world, the way government squanders our tax money.

The private sector pays for everything -- the firemen, cops, schoolteachers, and the sanitation department. It provides all the jobs for those who do not hold government jobs. And most important, the private sector pays the cost of our national defense. A worker in the private sector creates wealth. Workers in the public sector consume wealth.

Survival

CHAPTER XIV

Survival, reproduction, and acquiring knowledge all boil down to survival. The fishermen struggle against the sea. The commuter faces the dangers of highway accidents. We all face the threat of the sub-culture maggots who are dedicated to never doing anything constructive in their lives. Their creed is that we owe them a living and, by God, if we do not give it to them, they will take it from us one way or the other. In their minds they are right, for they are paranoid. The whole world is conspiring to keep them in poverty. When in actual fact, they have gotten the way they are because of the free ride the governments, at all levels, give them.

Make no mistake about it, just as maggots eat away at the healthy flesh of their host; they will ultimately destroy the creature they are feeding on. And the sub-culture of human maggots who are gnawing away at our nation will destroy us if they are not stopped.

The solution to the problem is to severely restrict government programs for the "needy".

Leonard Reed (late head of the *Foundation for Economic Education*) who made the same point to an audience of professors was castigated by a member in the audience for being callous toward the hungry and the starving.

"Have you ever seen anyone starve to death in America?" Reed asked.

"Yes", the professor answered. "I have seen two to three people starve to death."

"I refuse to believe that you would stand by and do nothing while two or three of your fellow humans starved to death," Reed replied.

Think about it. To the professor, starving is such a mundane occurrence that he was not sure if it was two or three people he had seen starve to death. Of course he had not seen anyone starve. He was trying to make Reed look like a fool, but ended by making himself the fool.

Think of the pedophile who ravaged the body of a child, and the horror the child experienced having been violated by such a monster. The pain must have been beyond description, and in many cases, death.

The solution to pedophilia is castration or life without parole. But, many will say, the punishment is too harsh. Once they have paid their debt to society (society? What is that? How about the victim?) They should be given their freedom. Sure, and give them another child to ravage. After all, look at the suffering they went through while in prison, deprived of sex. As Bob Elliot of Channel 6 in Portland, Maine, use to say, "Ain't that odd."

******

What about wars? As a teenager I was a flight engineer on a B-24 in the 5th Air Force. Since then, I have seen all kinds of wars, including the present war on terrorism. All the wars in my lifetime and in the history of the world have been people killing people. On the ocean I have never seen lobsters waging war against lobsters, nor ground fish, nor any other ocean species. And the same can be said for all land animals, except for us "humans".

Through the centuries, wars have eliminated millions upon millions of men, women, and children. The population of earth is substantially less because of humans slaughtering humans. As pointed out earlier, could this be Nature's way of controlling the human population?

The fishermen control the lobster population in a limited way. Ground fish, such as Cod, Haddock, Pollock, several other predators, and sea birds consume many times more lobsters than the fishermen can harvest.

Nature controls population by balancing population and available food. When a species thrives because of plentiful food, the food supply becomes depleted and then those that fed on the bounty become much fewer in number. The depleted food supply recovers, and those that fed on it do the same. The cycle repeats itself over and over again.

Most creatures will fight to protect their territory and will even encroach on their neighbor's ground. If they get away with it, they increase their chances of survival.

Hitler types are not happy with encroachment. Such types want the whole world. None have ever succeeded, but that does not keep the animal people from trying. At this moment in time, it is the radical Muslims who are taking a turn at subjugating all of us. Be a Muslim, or be dead, take your pick. Here is the solution to this problem. Take the corpses of all Muslim radicals who are killed in combat and the suicide bombers' body parts and bury them with dead pigs. Put a live pig in the cargo bays of all jetliners, trains, cargo containers, and commuter vehicles. The terrorists are willing to die and go to heaven with a busload of their very own virgins. I will bet they're not willing to do the same and end up in hell with a dead pig as a sexual partner.

Inside Myself

CHAPTER XV

"Inside myself is a place where I live
all alone and that's where you renew
your springs that never dry up."

Pearl Buck

I spend most of my time in that quiet place. I love it there. It is calm -- no noise pollution. No one ever disagrees with me. I am always right. Even when I am not sure of the answer to a problem, it's not a problem because I know, in time, I will find the answer.

Every trap I haul, in this quiet place, is full! I can reach into the trap with my eyes closed and never get bitten. I get five, no, ten pounds per trap, and the boat price is ten dollars per pound!

The sea is flat calm in this quiet place, and the bait is still fresh. There is no need to replace it. I am never more than an hour from home. I can see within myself, that the thieves and hog liners are coming up empty with every trap they haul. And there is Sam, the bastard. He is calling for help. His engine has quit. I will give him a tow back to port and give him a chance to see the fabulous catch I have. That will drive him out of his mind with envy. He cannot show his anger. He has to smile and pretend that he is pleased with my success. After all, I am his ticket to safety. I have to sympathize with his plight for someday the shoe might be on the other foot. I would not want Sam, the bastard, to think I do not consider him a "friend".

In my quiet place within myself my wife always smiles and never makes a sound. I, in turn, never do anything dumb. The children always obey and brush their teeth without being told and without breaking the silence.

IF IT DOESN'T IMPROVE ON SILENCE, THEN ONE SHOULD STAY QUIET.

(Maine wisdom.)

"Inside myself is a place where I live all alone," and yet I am never lonely, nor bored. I am calm. I can feel my nerves relax. My muscles do the same. I have my own mute button. If I do not want to hear it, with a push of the button, it is gone!

It's like sitting on the shore of the Gut at Biddeford Pool (a narrow channel that feeds and drains the Back Bay with each change of tide.). The only sounds I hear are the gentle flow of water and the Eider ducks streaking by at great speeds, a few inches above the water. At times, the loudest noise is the Eiders' wings striking the water as one of them struggles to become airborne. Whether I am within myself, or out in the world of reality, this is my favorite spot on earth.

In the private world of my inner self I am free to walk on the ocean bottom. I can greet and talk to the lobsters. I can see the great numbers of traps and the multitude of lobsters and fish of all kinds. The bottom is littered with lost and storm-destroyed gear. It provides shelter for many of the bottom dwellers. It is good that this mess is not visible from the surface. The ocean would be an eyesore rather than the thing of beauty that it is. In time the ocean will heal itself, and the scrap will disappear. In time I, too, will disappear.

For now, I am still here. In that special place, within myself, I look back at the many years at sea. I also look back at my years of flying, driving stockcars and dragsters and eighteen wheelers, the sports I have excelled at, the thousands of words I have written, and the true friends, male and female, who I have known. As I look back, I notice that all of the pleasant things come to mind. The pain is there, but, somehow, it is barely visible.

I am now nearly at the end of my struggle to survive. I can see it. As the wounded lobster with its will to survive as strong as ever, its lost strength will not allow it to succeed. It does not know it is doomed to failure, but I do.

My wife says I am "as deaf as a post". Actually, I am in a different place than she. I am looking into my future. Survival is important, but not as important as it once was. Problems multiply. The body begins to break down. The ability to defend myself is gone. If I had to run to save myself, I could not do it.

******

In this place within, I see a lightly overcast sky. The ocean reflects a light shade of gray. There is no wind. The nearly flat-calm sea is disturbed by gentle swells of one to two feet.

I can see my body, naked, face down in the water. There is no chill to the water, neither is it warm. As it washes over my body, it massages my flesh. It is pleasant. As I inhale the ocean air, it pleases the senses, as only one who has spent many years at sea can appreciate. I am swimming away from shore ever so slowly. As each swell passes over my head, I take another breath. The fragrance of each breath passes through my body. It calms me. It thrills me. It excites my being and condenses a lifetime within Nature's womb into a single breath.

The swells are taller now. I am a long way from shore. It is no longer possible to breathe between each oncoming sea. My naked body is unencumbered by civilized-imposed garments. It keeps moving through the sea, nearly parallel to the surface -- five feet, ten feet, twenty feet below the gentle swells.

My body is part of the sea. In slow motion it will travel from the area of Wood Island Light, through Bigelow Bight, south to Cape Cod. Then from Cape Cod it will move farther out to sea and head east to Amen Ledge, and then to Nova Scotia.

It will then be carried by the tide, back to Maine. The tidal currents along the Maine coast will move it to the point of origin -- the waters of Biddeford, Maine.

I will repeat this journey onto infinity in the company of the thousands of mariners "lost at sea". Our souls will make the journey together and will be calmed by the years at sea and our life experiences.

Look down into the waters of the Gulf of Maine. It is gray. The visibility is only a few feet. There are those who argue it is plankton. It is not. It is the ghost of my father, sisters, and generation upon generation of fishermen. Eventually, I will join them. I, too, will rest in peace, deep in Nature's womb where all life begins. Here we will survive forever.

THE END

www.ingramcontent.com/pod-product-compliance
Lightning Source LLC
Chambersburg PA
CBHW070013110426
42741CB00034B/1622